MENTORING
NEW
TEACHERS

MENTORING
NEW
TEACHERS

Hal Portner
Foreword by
Gerald N. Tirozzi

CORWIN PRESS, INC.
A Sage Publications Company
Thousand Oaks, California

For information:

Corwin Press, Inc.
A Sage Publications Company
2455 Teller Road
Thousand Oaks, California 91320
E-mail: order@corwinpress.com

SAGE Publications Ltd.
6 Bonhill Street
London EC2A 4PU
United Kingdom

SAGE Publications India Pvt. Ltd.
M-32 Market
Greater Kailash I
New Delhi 110 048 India

Printed in the United States of America

Library of Congress Cataloging-in-Publication Data

Portner, Hal.
    Mentoring new teachers / Hal Portner.
      p. cm.
    ISBN 0-8039-6714-4 (cloth: acid-free paper)
    ISBN 0-8039-6715-2 (pbk: acid-free paper)
    1. Mentoring in education—United States. 2. First year teachers—United States. 3. Teachers—In-service training—United States.   I. Title.
    LB1731.4 .P67 1998
    370′.71′5—ddc21   98-19774

This book is printed on acid-free paper.

98 99 00 01 02 03 10 9 8 7 6 5 4 3 2 1

Production Editor: S. Marlene Head
Editorial Assistant: Kristen L. Gibson
Typesetter: Rebecca Evans
Cover Designer: Michelle Lee

Contents

Foreword

Hal Portner has a long and impressive career in the field of education. His background as a teacher, school district administrator, state Department of Education staff member, and consultant in higher education presents him as an educator eminently qualified to address the important issues underlying the preparation and induction of new teachers.

I had the pleasure of working closely with Mr. Portner in my role as Connecticut's Commissioner of Education (1983-1991). He played a key role in the implementation of the state's Education Enhancement Act, passed in 1986, which dramatically raised teacher salaries as standards for the profession. In particular, he assisted in designing and implementing professional development activities and programs, and the mentorship and induction model for new teachers. He also served as the coordinator of the Connecticut Institute for Teaching and Learning—which became Connecticut's major vehicle and catalyst for offering comprehensive, sustained professional development for teachers and administrators.

It is gratifying for me to see Mr. Portner utilize his expertise and "hands-on" involvement in writing a timely, instructive, and important book on mentoring new teachers. The book provides direction and guidance that clearly outlines how to be a mentor. The important areas of coaching, guiding, relating, and assessing are presented within a conceptual and practical framework. In effect, the author provides a "workbook" approach in the mentorship learning process, which draws the reader into an interactive mode. Mr. Portner's efforts are "user friendly."

The reader will be impressed with the author's practical and concrete suggestions and recommendations, his reference to a variety of techniques, and his use of learning style inventories. The various techniques described are presented in an open-ended manner, challenging the reader to further explore and expand on the myriad ideas presented.

This book will be of great service and utility to teachers who are presently serving as mentors, as well as teachers who are considering their involvement as mentors of teachers. School administrators, especially school principals, will benefit from the book as they plan induction and orientation programs for new staff, as well as the potential to engage more teachers as role models and "guides" for those new to the profession. Teacher-educators will find Mr. Portner's work a valuable resource or supplementary text in supervision and evaluation courses.

The induction of new teachers is arguably the most important component of a long-term comprehensive model of teacher growth and development. Regardless of the quality of the preparation of a first-year teacher, it is ultimately that initial day, week, month, and year that often predict success or failure in the classroom. Quality mentorship by experienced teachers can serve to provide much needed support, assistance, and guidance in the formative years of teaching. To this end, Mr. Portner has made a significant contribution to the profession of teaching.

DR. GERALD N. TIROZZI

Preface

B ecause you are reading this, I assume that you are someone who is a mentor; someone who is going to be doing some mentoring; someone who hasn't yet decided whether you want to be a mentor; someone who trains and/or otherwise supports mentors; someone who has or would like to have a mentor (that would make you a mentee); or someone who is just plain curious about mentoring.

Not many years ago, few educators would have fit into any of the above categories. Mentoring—if it existed at all in the culture of a school—was initiated either as an informal response to a new teacher seeking help or as assistance offered to a new teacher by an experienced colleague willing to share his or her expertise. In contrast, other professionals, like doctors and lawyers, and tradespeople, like plumbers and electricians, have been inducted into their respective fields through formal internships or by serving as apprentices "paying their dues"—both examples of programs in which novices are formally paired with mentors.

Since the early 1980s, however, more and more educational policy makers and leaders have come to recognize that mentoring is a powerful and effective way to provide support and assistance to neophyte teachers during their first year on the job. In July of 1997, *The Seven Priorities of the U.S. Department of Education* was published as a working document detailing the initiatives of the Secretary of Education. Priority Five of that document identifies six areas that affect the quality of teachers. One of these areas, the fourth, stresses the need for "special efforts to retain beginning teachers in their first few years of teaching, because we now lose 30% due to a lack of support." Also in 1997, President Clinton issued his *Call to Action for American Education in the 21st Century,* in which he advocates "a talented and dedicated teacher in every classroom" and encourages school districts to "make sure that beginning teachers get support and mentoring from experienced teachers." To date, more than 30 states have mandated some form of mentoring support for beginning teachers.

Who Should Read This Book

I have written this book primarily for the person who already is a mentor and wants to hone his or her skills, who is going to be doing some mentoring and wants to do it well, or who hasn't yet decided whether to be a mentor and wants to know more about what mentors do.

Mentoring New Teachers is intended as 1) a self-instruction, how-to workbook for a serving or prospective mentor; 2) a sourcebook for participants in (and leaders of) mentor training programs; 3) a supplementary text for a seminar or a graduate-level course in educational leadership; and 4) a practical resource for a school district's administrators, as well as staff development coordinator and committee members. Its focus is on the mentoring behaviors associated with four critical mentoring functions: Relating, Assessing, Coaching, and Guiding. A series of exercises, supplemented by anecdotes, commentary, and example, spans several chapters. I have designed these exercises to help the reader develop practical mentoring behaviors and construct his or her own understanding of the critical mentoring functions.

Overview of the Contents

I have organized the elements of what it takes to be a successful mentor of new teachers into eight components: an introduction that sets the stage, four chapters that present the details of what mentors do, a fifth chapter that suggests ways to tweak the mentoring environment, and two resources that provide rich supplementary materials. After reading this book and working through its exercises, you will have gained a comprehensive perspective of mentoring, a set of basic mentoring skills, and a variety of practical strategies for applying mentoring's functional behaviors.

The introduction discusses what mentors do and why. It elicits from your own experience the behaviors you consider to be consistent with good mentoring. Four critical mentoring functions—Relating, Assessing, Coaching, and Guiding—are introduced. The introduction emphasizes the importance of training experienced teachers to use the behaviors associated with these functions and clarifies the differences, as well as similarities, between mentoring and supervising.

Chapter 1, "Relating," stresses the important part a relationship plays in the mentoring process. Through a set of introspective exercises, you learn ways to establish trust and to pay attention to such nonverbal communication as thoughts, feelings, and body language—behaviors that help build and maintain a professionally productive relationship with a mentee.

Chapter 2, "Assessing," provides you with a variety of ways to gather and diagnose data about a mentee's teaching, learning, and acculturation needs. Exercises and suggestions help you determine how your mentee receives and processes information. The chapter describes how the assessing function can help you make informed mentoring decisions.

Chapter 3, "Coaching," familiarizes you with classroom observation and pre- and postobservation conferencing strategies. A series of exercises clarifies and provides the opportunity to practice behaviors that you need to help a mentee reflect on his or her performance and make decisions about his or her teaching.

Chapter 4, "Guiding," provides ways to wean a mentee from dependence on a mentor. The chapter systematically guides you through the process of directing a mentee's journey from unseasoned neophyte to self-reliant practitioner. It discusses and provides opportunities to practice diagnosing a mentee's level of ability and motivation in relation to a given situation, and to use appropriate behaviors to both address the situation and move the mentee to a higher level.

Chapter 5, "Tips and Observations," suggests some things you can do to make mentoring more effective and more gratifying.

The resources at the end of the book include (A) an annotated bibliography of selected publications that supplement the material covered in this book and (B) the Connecticut Competency Instrument (CCI), which describes the teaching competencies expected of a beginning teacher that are observable in the teacher's classroom.

Acknowledgments

It is with a great deal of gratitude and appreciation that I acknowledge the time, energy, and considerable expertise the following colleagues devoted to the critical review of this manuscript. Their comments, suggestions, and insights were most appropriate and many were incorporated into the final version.

- Christine L. Brown, Director of Foreign Languages, Connecticut Public School District
- Kaye Dean, Elementary School Principal, Arizona
- Norma Gluck, Regent Emeritus, New York State Department of Education
- Dr. Robert Pauker, Educational Consultant
- Murray Schuman, Dean of Social Sciences, Holyoke (Massachusetts) Community College

I also wish to thank my wife, Mary, for her patience and support, and Dr. Gerald N. Tirozzi, Assistant Secretary for Elementary and Secondary Education at the U.S. Department of Education, for his advice, encouragement, and friendship over the years.

HAL PORTNER
Northampton, Massachusetts
March, 1998

About the Author

Hal Portner is a certified and experienced K-12 teacher and administrator. He was Assistant Director of the SummerMath Program for High School Women and Teachers, Mount Holyoke College, and for 14 years was a teacher and administrator in a Connecticut public school district. Portner holds an M.Ed. from the University of Michigan, a 6th-year CAGS in Education Administration from the University of Connecticut, and for 3 years was with the University of Massachusetts Ed.D. Educational Leadership Program. From 1985 to 1995, he was on the staff of the Connecticut State Department of Education, Bureau of Certification and Professional Development, where he worked closely with school districts to design and carry out professional development and teacher evaluation plans and programs. Among the major accomplishments of the Bureau was the development, implementation, and fine-tuning of Connecticut's Beginning Educator Support and Training (BEST) program, a nationally acclaimed beginning teacher mentoring and assessment initiative.

Portner writes, consults, and presents workshops for educational organizations and institutions. He currently serves as Consultant for Professional Development for the faculty and staff of a community college in Massachusetts where, among other responsibilities, he trains experienced faculty members to be mentors.

Introduction

Have you ever had a mentor? Someone—perhaps a college professor, family member, coworker, or friend—who inspired you, helped keep you going, and showed you the ropes? In the field of education, mentors are usually veteran teachers who support colleagues new to the profession, encourage them, and help them become better teachers.

Raymond is a veteran teacher. He was selected to become a mentor for a new colleague in his school. Raymond was excited about his new role. He was also nervous because he wanted to do a good job. Raymond decided to spend a few minutes thinking about others who had helped him when he began his teaching career. He made a list of those positive behaviors that helped him to become a better teacher and person.

I asked Raymond to share his list with me. I was curious what the people he considered to have been his mentors did that supported, encouraged, and helped him become the fine educator he is. Raymond's list is on the next page. But wait . . . before you turn the page, take a few minutes to think about those who mentored you. What are your recollections?

What are some things a person you consider to have been your mentor did that supported, encouraged, and helped you to grow professionally? Perhaps one thing that person did was celebrate your achievements in some way. Construct your own list. Write six of your mentor's positive behaviors in the space below.

_____   _____

_____   _____

_____   _____

Here is what Raymond remembers about his mentors:

They made themselves available.

They listened to what he had to say.

They were encouraging and optimistic.

They seemed to know what he needed and when he needed it.

They invited him to watch them teach, then discussed with him what they did and why they did it.

They were willing to share their expertise.

They helped him set realistic goals and timelines.

They made practical suggestions.

They directed him to other people or resources when they did not have answers.

They provided him with constructive and timely feedback on his planning and teaching.

They encouraged him to take risks and to make his own decisions.

They made him think about what he was doing in such a way that it helped him consider whether there were better ways.

They helped him feel that he was not on his own.

They believed in his ability to succeed.

In addition to Raymond's list, here are some attributes of good mentoring that others have shared with me. A colleague from the private sector lists these mentoring traits on the World Wide Web page, www.geocities.com/HotSprings/5891/:

A mentor looks for signs of specialness that he can somehow work with and develop.

A mentor manages to "think out loud" in the [mentee's] presence.

A mentor gives honest advice when needed.

A mentor does not let his [mentee] get beat up or spit out.

A mentor lets her [mentee] "shine." She knows the credit will reflect back on her as much as it does on the [mentee].

And from an elementary school principal, these observations:

> The mechanics of teaching can be taught, but the love for children cannot. Mentors who are able to communicate their caring for children are better mentors. . . . Because teaching is a new experience every time you walk into a classroom, good teachers build a repertoire of strategies and tools that they can use when they need them. Good mentors share their tools with their mentees and help them build their own repertoire.

Your list, Raymond's, and the others include a wide variety of mentoring behaviors. Successful mentors not only have an extensive repertoire of such behaviors but also use them appropriately when they interact with their mentees, when they attempt to figure out what their mentees need, when they guide their mentees' professional growth, and when they encourage their mentees to make informed decisions on their own. The protégés of successful mentors feel empowered and eventually become willing and able to identify and address their own professional problems and needs. And lo and behold, many successful mentors have discovered that when they employed behaviors that enabled their protégés to grow, their own competencies also strengthened!

Wide Support for Mentoring

In recognition of the promise mentoring holds as a vehicle for educational reform, more than 30 states have mandated beginning teacher support as part of their teacher induction programs. In response to the challenge imposed by these mandates, increasing numbers of school districts have arranged for experienced teachers to help their new colleagues persist and develop beyond their difficult first year.

Additionally, both the National Education Association and the American Federation of Teachers, the nation's largest teachers' unions, are in accord in their encouragement of the establishment of peer review and assistance programs under which all beginning teachers would be assigned a mentor.

Idealistic considerations aside, much of the recent support for mentoring new teachers can be attributed primarily to two practical factors. One of these is the high rate of attrition among new teachers. According to the 1996 report of the National Commission on Teaching and America's Future, up to one third of new teachers in the United States leave the profession within their first 3 years. One reason for this "wastage of teaching resources," according to the Commission, is "the country's typical 'sink-or-swim' attitude toward teacher induction." Successful teaching is an art that takes insight, knowledge, and many years of experience to develop, yet there are all too many instances where new teachers never remain in the profession long enough to develop the art of teaching because they have no initial or ongoing support base. Rather, according to the Commission's report, new teachers are literally "isolated behind classroom doors with little feedback or help . . . while others [even if they do not eventually drop out of teaching] learn merely to cope rather than to teach well."

A second reason educational leaders support mentoring is their recognition of the unprecedented number of veteran teachers who are nearing retirement. In Massachusetts, for example, by the Year 2000, more than 50% of public school teachers will have been in the classroom for more than 20 years. President Clinton, in his *Call to Action for American Education in the 21st Century*, points out that nationally, 2 million teachers will be needed during the next 10 years to replace retirees and accommodate rapidly growing student enrollment. The large number of new teachers entering the profession within the next few years will need support—the kind of support that mentors are expected to provide.

Successful Mentors Are Made, Not Born

In February 1997, the U.S. Department of Education's National Center for Education Statistics published its report, *Teacher Professionalization and Teacher Commitment: A Multilevel Analysis*. Among the findings of the study described in this report was that having a mentor program to assist beginning teachers is less important for improving teacher performance and commitment than the quality of that assistance.

So how can a school district see to it that its mentoring program is of high quality? Part of the answer is to give veteran classroom teachers the opportunity to be mentors. Experienced teachers generally take on the challenge and responsibility of mentoring with high hopes and good intentions. Classroom expertise, hope, and good intentions, however, will not by themselves guarantee effective and accomplished performance as a mentor. A dedicated, experienced teacher becomes an effective and accomplished mentor by design and training, not by chance.

Many educational leaders recognize the fallacy of assuming that veteran teachers, by virtue of years of successful experience in the classroom, automatically make good mentors for adults. Consequently, an increasing number of educational organizations at local, regional, and state levels are providing professional development opportunities for mentors. These efforts typically include distributing relevant reading materials to mentors, organizing mentoring conferences and seminars, and providing comprehensive mentoring workshops. Both the reading materials and the seminars generally aim to impart a body of knowledge germane to working with adult colleagues. This knowledge base includes such concepts as Stage Theory and Adult Development. Comprehensive workshops usually touch on these concepts and also provide opportunities for participants to learn and develop conferencing and classroom observation skills.

Acquiring the special knowledge and skills of mentoring is critical to the development of an effective mentor. However, there is an additional aspect to mentoring that perhaps does not receive enough emphasis. This subtle and sometimes overlooked facet of mentoring has to do with understanding the purpose and function of the mentor's role in relation to that of supervisor, curriculum coordinator, and department head.

Mentoring Is Not Evaluating

Consider this scenario. In your district, subject coordinators are expected to serve as mentors as well as supervisors to new teachers in their departments. You are a new teacher. Ana, your mentor-supervisor, calls you into her office and gives you a list of books to use for your classes. You are disappointed with the list because it does not offer the students a wide enough range of views. You and Ana have developed a good professional relationship in the short time you have been working together, and for the most part, you have found her advice and suggestions to be helpful. You would like to discuss your viewpoint about the book list, but a little twinge in the pit of your stomach reminds you that Ana soon will be filing an evaluation report on you with the principal, and you don't want to "rock the boat." You tuck the list into your pocket and walk away, trying to decide whether to accept the list and follow it closely or to substitute books of your own choosing on the sly.

A critical difference between the role of supervisor (e.g., department head, curriculum coordinator, or principal) and the role of mentor is that a mentor cannot be an evaluator. Trust and confidentiality are vital components of mentoring. It is virtually impossible for anyone—especially someone in a new environment trying to prove himself or herself—to expose insecurities and inexperience to a coworker and leave oneself vulnerable to possible ridicule and censure. Yet it may be necessary for a mentee to risk these behaviors in order to help the mentor understand the crux of a situation. This degree of openness may be difficult to achieve if it is the mentor's responsibility to evaluate the mentee or to recommend certification.

Here are some other distinctions between the role of mentor and evaluator.

- Mentoring is collegial; evaluating is hierarchical.
- Mentoring is ongoing; evaluating visits are set by policy.
- Mentoring develops self-reliance; evaluating judges performance.
- Mentoring keeps data confidential; evaluating files it and makes it available.
- Mentoring uses data to reflect; evaluating uses it to judge.
- In mentoring, value judgments are made by the teacher; in evaluation, they are made by the supervisor.

There are, of course, some commonalties between the roles of mentor and supervisor. For example, the mentor shares with his or her supervising colleagues the goal of improving the quality of the novice's teaching, often attempting to achieve that goal by helping the beginner to develop lesson plans, to select curriculum materials, and to construct assessment tools. But an effective mentor understands that improving classroom performance is not enough, that it is also a function of mentoring to stimulate the mentee's own critical and creative thinking about how to teach and how children learn. It is the evaluation aspect of supervision that is contrary to the basic nature of mentoring.

The Mentor's Primary Role

It is simplistic to think of a mentor as a guru, a master teacher, at whose feet one sits and to whom one poses occasional questions, hoping to absorb the mysteries of the art. The role of mentor as "expert-who-has-the-answers" has its place and value, but a new teacher needs to develop the capacity and confidence to make his or her own informed decisions, enrich his or her own knowledge, and sharpen his or her own abilities regarding teaching and learning. Purposefully bringing a mentee to this level of professionalism is the mentor's primary role.

A mentor functions best in this role by relating, assessing, coaching, and guiding. These four functions draw upon the eclectic body of knowledge that informs the mentoring process and are carried out through a variety of skills and behaviors.

What Mentors Do: The Four Mentoring Functions

Relating

Mentors build and maintain relationships with their mentees based on mutual trust, respect, and professionalism. Relating behaviors create an environment that allows mentors to develop a genuine understanding of their mentees' ideas and needs and encourages mentees to honestly share and reflect upon their experiences.

Assessing

Mentors gather and diagnose data about their mentees' ways of teaching and learning; they determine their mentees' competency and confidence to handle a given situation; they identify unique aspects of the school and community culture; and they take note of the school district's formal and informal procedures and practices. Assessing behaviors ensure that the mentees' professional needs are identified so that mentoring decisions can be based on a thoughtful consideration of a variety of data.

Coaching

Mentors help their mentees fine-tune their professional skills, enhance their grasp of subject matter, locate and acquire resources, and expand their repertoire of teaching modalities. Coaching behaviors allow mentors to serve as role models to their mentees; to share relevant experiences, examples and strategies; and especially to open new avenues by which mentees can, through reflection and practice, take responsibility for improving their own teaching.

Guiding

Mentors wean their mentees away from dependence by guiding them through the process of reflecting on decisions and actions for themselves and encouraging them to construct their own informed teaching and learning approaches. Teaching involves constant decision making. The mentor places the responsibility for decision making with the mentee. Decisions about teaching are driven by reflection. The guiding skill of the mentor is to ask the right questions the right way, and at the right time—questions that encourage the mentee to reflect on his or her decisions. Guiding behaviors stimulate the mentees' creative and critical thinking, empower them to envision future situations, encourage them to take informed risks, and help them build the capacity to develop perceptive decisions and take appropriate actions.

These mentoring functions do not occur in isolation. They consistently overlap and complement each other during the mentoring process.

Functions and behaviors aside, ultimately, a successful mentor must possess an additional attribute—one that is fundamental to mentoring's primary purpose. When all is said and done, a mentor, upon reflecting on his or her mentoring experience, must see himself or herself as having been not only a master teacher who may have had some answers, but also one who acted on the belief that learning takes place best between and among colleagues exploring together. This book is written in that spirit.

Relating

1

Kevin had always wanted to teach, and now he had landed his first teaching job. In spite of his excellent student teaching experience, he found himself overwhelmed by the activities and responsibilities of the first few weeks. The formal orientation to the school and bus tour of the town helped a little, but for the most part, he felt that he was operating in the classroom without sufficient information and with little support.

He had been assigned a "mentor," Katherine Pelletier. Katherine was an experienced teacher who, Kevin was told, would help him through the first few months. Kevin met Katherine briefly during orientation. "Don't worry, you'll do just fine," she told him. "We'll set up a schedule of meetings to discuss how I can be of help to you. Meanwhile, don't hesitate to come see me any time you have any questions."

Even though Kevin did have questions and occasionally experienced feelings of insecurity, he was reluctant to burden his mentor with his problems. When they had their first meeting, Kevin glossed over the difficulties he was having with class management—after all, he did not want to appear incompetent. Katherine Pelletier was aware of his problems with classroom discipline, but not wanting to give the impression that she was a "prying know-it-all," she too avoided the topic. Consequently, although Kevin and Katherine met regularly and exchanged pleasantries, they never did have a meaningful discussion about his classroom management concerns or, for that matter, about any other such issue. It was no surprise, then, that the first few months of teaching were somewhat chaotic for Kevin.

Mentoring requires interaction. But in order to be productive, mentor-mentee interactions must take place within a relationship that includes mutual trust, honesty, respect, and a joyful willingness to work together. It is important to build and maintain a productive mentor-mentee relationship because it provides the mechanism for—and is the source of energy behind—a mentor's ability to carry out the other mentoring functions.

Unless a solid working relationship is established from the start, the mentoring process runs the risk of being like that experienced by Kevin and Katherine: perfunctory and carried out merely as routine. Even if a relationship is initially well established, it needs to be maintained. Otherwise, over time, interactions between mentor and mentee will tend to deteriorate into workaday obligations. Therefore, your first, and potentially most challenging, responsibility as a mentor is to develop and maintain a productive relationship with your mentee.

So how do you go about developing and maintaining a productive mentoring relationship—one that you and your mentee will cherish as an opportunity for collegial interchange and professional growth? In this chapter, we will explore three powerful sets of behaviors—establishing trust, paying attention to thoughts and feelings, and being sensitive to nonverbal communication—that can help you build a beneficial collegial relationship with your mentee.

Establishing Trust

Before we consider how to build trust in a mentor-mentee relationship—and why trust is an important part of that relationship—we need to be clear as to what constitutes trust. What does trust mean to you? What is it like to be in a relationship where trust exists? In what ways do you relate differently to a person you trust from the way you relate to someone you do not particularly trust? The following exercise will help answer these questions.

Exercise 1.1 *How you act when you trust*

Think about someone you know and trust. Keep that person in mind as you complete the following sentence:

"Because I trust (the person you have in mind), I . . . "

(List several behaviors, feelings, thoughts and expectations you experience because you trust that person.)

Note: I've done this exercise too, but don't peek at my list on the next
page until you have created your own in the space above. There are
no "right" answers, of course, because we all have our own perception of trust. I am sharing my list just to provide another viewpoint.

Here is my list: "When I trust Mary, I . . . "

"freely share my experiences and my aspirations."

"tend to use humor more often."

"listen to and respect her opinions, even though I may disagree."

"will ask for and appreciate her opinion and advice."

"will lend or give her a cherished possession."

"try to understand her meanings and intent by probing for more information."

"am willing to offer more information if asked."

"feel at ease with her."

"feel comfortable asking her for help."

Now that you and I have more or less defined trust in terms of its associated behaviors, the next question we need to answer in keeping with our focus on building a productive mentor-mentee relationship is how to get your mentee to trust you.

Exercise 1.2 Behaviors that elicit trust

Complete the following sentence:

"When I want someone to trust me, I . . . "(List several behaviors you exhibit when you want someone to trust you.)

_____

_____

_____

_____

_____

_____

Note: Yes, I have developed a list for this exercise also. It is on the following page. Wait, don't turn the page yet. Complete your list first.

Here is my list: "When I want someone to trust me, I . . . "

> "walk the talk; that is, I do what I said I would do." As a friend of mine puts it, "trust is the residue of promises kept."

> "respect confidentiality."

> "respond to his or her statements and questions to his or her satisfaction before introducing another topic."

> "express my feelings as well as my thoughts."

> "recognize and respect his or her feelings and ideas, even though I may not agree with them."

Now, between your lists and mine, we have a litany of trust-building behaviors.

Why is trust so important an ingredient in a relationship? It is important because it allows both the mentor and mentee to recognize, accept, discuss, and consequently work to improve ineffective practices. After all, it takes trust to ask for help, to expose your insecurities and inexperience to a coworker, and to leave yourself vulnerable and open to ridicule. It may well be necessary for your mentee to risk these behaviors in order to help you understand the crux of a situation.

Paying Attention to
Thoughts and Feelings

Do you remember what was going through your mind and the emotions you experienced that first day on the job as a teacher? Too many years ago? Well then, how about a more recent situation—like when you first thought about being a mentor. The following exercise may help you recall that occasion.

Exercise 1.3 Relive the experience

When the possibility of being a mentor first occurred to you, do you remember what it felt like? What were some of your concerns, thoughts and feelings?

Read the following scenarios. As you read, try to recall some of the thoughts and feelings you had when you first considered being a mentor. Jot down your reflections in the space provided on page 17.

Scene 1: Gloria Jackson, a high school biology teacher, picks up the memo she found in her school mail box this morning. It reads:

```
MEMO TO: Gloria Jackson

FROM: Building Principal

RE: Invitation to mentor a new teacher

Several new teachers will be joining our staff
when the school year begins next fall. As you know,
the district has recently instituted a Beginning
Teacher Support Program that matches newly hired
teachers with experienced ones. I feel you would
make an excellent Mentor for one of our new col-
leagues. Please come to my office during your
scheduled free period next Tuesday when we can
discuss details.
```

Gloria opens her scheduling book and enters a note about meeting with the principal on the following Tuesday.

Scene 2: Next Tuesday, Gloria's free period. She rereads the memo, tucks it into her scheduling book, tucks the scheduling book under her arm, and heads toward the principal's office.

"Me, a mentor?" she thinks to herself as she walks down the hall. "Hey, why not! The principal thinks I can do it. After all, good mentoring is probably very much like good teaching. Here is my chance to help a new teacher by passing on what I've learned over the past 10 years."

"I am looking forward to being an 'official' mentor. I've helped beginning teachers before, but I've never really had the formal responsibility. But what if I do a poor job? How will I feel about myself? What will others think of me?"

"Hey, why am I worrying? I'm good at what I do. I know how to teach; I have good rapport with my students and colleagues."

"I remember back when I first started teaching. I had doubts about whether I would ever become a competent teacher, let alone survive my first year in the classroom. I really felt that I was on my own. I did make it finally, but I sure wish I had someone there for me, someone I felt comfortable with. I guess a mentor is someone that I could call on when I needed help, information or just reassurance."

"I know I should be more confident. I've heard and read enough about mentoring new teachers to understand what's involved. So why do I feel so apprehensive?"

"There are so many questions I have. When I meet with the principal, I'm sure some of these questions will be answered, but will the new teacher—my mentee—and I get along? I probably will get to watch my mentee teach, but how would I feel about having him or her watch me teach? There must be some expertise a mentor needs beyond experience as a practitioner and good interpersonal skills. What are they? Do I have them? If not, will I have the opportunity to acquire them?"

Gloria reaches the principal's office and enters with a mixture of anticipation and trepidation.

_____

_____

_____

_____

_____

_____

_____

_____

Did any of Gloria's reactions to taking on that new role resonate with ones you experienced at the time? If you, a veteran teacher like Gloria Jackson, experienced both anticipation and trepidation when faced with a new and important professional challenge, imagine what it must be like for a new teacher today. In addition to the many complex issues you probably faced when you became an educator, today's first-year teacher—your mentee—will be working from day one with an increasingly diverse student population and probably facing the challenge of integrating students with special needs into his or her classroom.

Your mentee will have questions about such issues as teaching, learning, school policy, and the community. Your mentee will also have thoughts and feelings about those aspects of his or her new profession. He or she will probably ask the questions, but unless you have developed a relationship with a history of attending to relevant thoughts and feelings, the discussion runs the risk of producing only superficial information from your mentee, thus allowing you only limited insight into the gist of the question. In other words, thoughts and feelings add depth to communication.

A powerful way to build and maintain a productive mentoring relationship is to share thoughts and feelings about teaching. It is important that you really listen to what your mentee tells you—not just to the words, but also to the feelings.

For example, responding to the following statement from your mentee: "I will be teaching exactly what I had hoped for—sixth grade math and science," with: "It sounds as though you're excited about meeting your students and getting started," will show the mentee that he or she is being heard at a deeper level than just the content of the words. Once those feelings have been addressed and accepted, the way may well be open for the mentee to voluntarily provide additional information and express some concerns that he or she was not comfortable doing before. So, not only is this attention to feelings helpful to the development of a good relationship, it also is an excellent way to draw out the mentee's specific needs and concerns.

Of course, you could just come right out and ask the new teacher what needs or concerns he or she has about teaching math and science to sixth graders, and you may get some useful information. But until the mentee trusts that feelings will be heard and honored, it may be difficult for a beginning teacher to risk exposing any insecurities to a stranger. Indeed, such a direct question—no matter how well intended—may even provoke additional feelings of insecurity.

By way of illustration, suppose that Sharon is Maureen's mentor. Sharon sits next to Maureen in the teacher's room one morning before school, nods a good morning to her mentee, and asks, "How are your classes going? You're working on writing, aren't you?"

"Oh, the students are writing O.K.," Maureen replies, "but I wish they would pay more attention to spelling."

"Don't worry about that," says Sharon. "Their spelling will improve in time. Can I get you a cup of coffee?"

Maureen sighs, "No, thanks. I had some earlier."

Sharon did not do a very good job of mentoring here, did she? Let's back up and consider what she could have said to acknowledge feelings, build trust, and encourage Maureen to consider a wider range of options.

When Maureen said, "The students are writing O.K., but I wish they would pay more attention to spelling," Sharon should have let Maureen know that she was aware of the feelings beneath the words by saying, for example, "It sounds as though you are concerned about your students' poor spelling. Go on, tell me more."

As their conversation progressed, Sharon should have periodically checked out her understanding of what Maureen was saying by restating in her own words what she and heard (e.g., "If I hear you correctly, you are saying that . . . " "Let's see if I understand you. Are you saying . . . " "When you said . . . , it seemed you were implying . . . "). Sharon then would have allowed Maureen to correct, clarify, or validate her restatement.

Suppose Maureen asks, "Do you think I should assign the students extra homework in spelling?"

Sometimes it is effective to answer a question with another question. This encourages your mentee to probe for his or her own answer. The questions you ask should be open-ended in that they require more than a "yes," "no," or other one-word answer. Starting your question with "why" or "how" will serve this purpose. How do you think Sharon should respond to Maureen's question about assigning extra spelling homework?

Here are some other relating behaviors that Sharon, the mentor, would find productive:

- Use descriptive rather than evaluative or judgmental statements. For example, if she is giving feedback to Maureen, her mentee, about how Maureen disciplined a disruptive student, Sharon might begin by saying, "I noticed that you took a big breath just before going over to talk to (the disruptive student)."
- When her mentee says or indicates something to her, Sharon needs to be aware that Maureen expects her response to be relevant to what she just said. By not honoring that expectation, Sharon risks cutting off further discussion of that topic, inhibiting further discussion in general, and eroding a little of the relationship.
- Occasionally, Sharon should check out the accuracy of any assumptions she may have about her mentee's unspoken thoughts or feelings. She can do this by paraphrasing back to her mentee what it is she assumes and allowing her to confirm or clarify.
- Above all, Sharon must—as all mentors must—respect confidentiality.

Communicating Nonverbally

Suppose you run into someone you haven't seen in a while and the person smiles and says to you, "So tell me, how are you, and what have you been up to lately?" Before you can answer, the smile disappears, the person glances at his or her watch, and then starts looking around, but not at you. Which message do you trust? What feelings are being expressed? I don't know about you, but to me the nonverbal message would come across much more strongly than the spoken words.

There is power in body language. When gestures and words conflict, confusion enters the relationship; when they are in harmony, trust is communicated and perceived.

Notice your mentee's facial expressions and general posture while he or she is speaking to you. Is he or she relaxed? Tense? Distracted? Even when a person's demeanor seems to be in sync with their words, the way he or she sits or moves can add other dimensions to what is being said at the time.

You may want to check out the accuracy of how you perceive your mentee's nonverbal expressions. Doing so will give your mentee the opportunity to clarify and perhaps to expand upon his or her comments. Keep in mind, however, that in and of itself, a specific body movement or expression does not necessarily indicate a specific meaning. Nonverbal cues should be considered together with other gestures and in context with spoken words. In addition, there are regional and cultural variations in the use and meaning of gestures and expressions that need to be considered. In general, however, most people will take someone leaning toward them while they are talking as meaning, "I am hearing you and interested in what you are saying." Crossed arms, by contrast, may connote discomfort with—or rejection of—an idea.

To what extent are you aware of the reactions your use of body language evokes in others? For example, when you are listening to your mentee and nod your head occasionally, chances are he or she feels that you are really paying attention to his or her words. The following exercise will show you the power of body language.

Exercise 1.4 *The power of body language*

When you find yourself in the kinds of situations described below, try using the body language I suggest and see what happens. In each of the two scenarios, notice that you consciously change or shift from one position to another. Take note of any changes in the content and quality of conversation that occurs after you shift. If your mentee is the other person in this exercise, be sure to explain, after it is over, what you were doing and why. You share this information with your mentee in order to reinforce trust and to dispel any misunderstanding that may have occurred. It would be advantageous to have the exercises videotaped, if doing so would not interfere with the activity, because it would be helpful to review the interactions from the viewpoint of an uninvolved observer.

Situation A: During a conversation, the other person begins telling you about something that happened earlier. Lean slightly toward the speaker. Look at the him or her with interest. Occasionally, nod your head.

In the middle of one of the speaker's sentences, shift. Lean back, look away and cross your arms. If the speaker asks you whether anything is wrong (or words to that effect) answer, "Oh, no. Please continue," but keep your body language aloof.

Situation B: During a conversation, you notice that the other person is sitting rather stiffly with fingers clasped together or grasping the arms of the chair. His or her feet are planted squarely on the floor, and he or she appears somewhat uncomfortable. Mirror the other's manner; assume the same posture and demeanor.

Early into the conversation, begin to gradually shift your body. First, unclasp your fingers. Wait for a corresponding relaxation of hands by the other person, then cross one leg over the other toward the person. Continue gradually moving your body into a more relaxed position, making slight changes each time your colleague mirrors you last adjustment.

When you carry out this exercise, you will probably notice that your body language communicated strong messages and elicited definite responses. In conversations with your mentee, if your words are honest, your body language will automatically reinforce what you say and contribute to the development of trust in your relationship.

Unless proven otherwise, trust that your mentee will be honest with you, will follow through with what he or she has agreed to do, and will honor the commitment made to the mentoring process. Your behaviors must engender the same level of trust in your mentee.

A Checklist of Relating Behaviors

✔ To the best of your ability, do you do what you say you will do?

✔ If you find that you cannot follow through on a promise, do you let your mentee know, and suggest an alternative?

✔ Unless given permission by your mentee, do you treat in confidence anything of a personal or professional nature that he or she tells you or you observe? (Of course, you will need to use your judgment in the event the situation involves a matter of safety, endangerment, or professional malpractice.)

✔ When your mentee offers some information or opinion, or asks a question, do you respond to his or her statement or query before going on to another topic?

✔ Where you feel comfortable doing so, do you express your feelings as well as thoughts about a topic under discussion?

✔ Do you acknowledge and respect your mentee's feelings and ideas, even though you may not agree with them?

✔ Do you probe for thoughts and feelings as well as facts when discussing professional issues?

✔ When your mentee offers some important information, do you encourage your mentee to say more in more detail?

✔ Do you periodically check out your assumptions about what your mentee was thinking and feeling as well as what was said? (You can do this by restating in your own words what you heard and assumed, and then allowing your mentee to correct, clarify, or validate your restatement.)

✔ Do you respect your mentee's ability to make decisions by encouraging him or her to probe for his or her own answers?

✔ Do you use descriptive rather than evaluative or judgmental statements when reviewing a mentee's decision or behavior?

✔ Do you let your body language reinforce the intent of your words?

✔ Are you sensitive to mixed messages—contradictory words and gestures—both from yourself and from your mentee? (You can avoid sending conflicting messages by being honest in what you say.)

✔ If you think you perceive disharmony between words and body movement, do you check out your assumptions and give your mentee the opportunity to clarify?

A Mentoring Relationship
Is a Serving Relationship

Rachel Naomi Remen, Assistant Clinical Professor of Family and Community Medicine at the University of California, San Francisco, in a talk given at the "Open Heart, Open Mind" conference in San Diego, California, in July 1995, made an observation about the care-

giving relationship that applies equally to the mentoring relationship. She said, "Serving is different from helping. Helping is based
on inequality; it is not a relationship between equals. . . . Helping
incurs debt. When you help someone they owe you one. But serving,
like healing, is mutual. There is no debt. I am as served as the person
I am serving. When I help I have a feeling of satisfaction. When I
serve I have a feeling of gratitude. These are very different things."
Ms. Remen went on to say, "Serving is also different from fixing.
When I fix a person I perceive them as broken. There is distance between ourselves and whatever or whomever we are fixing [and] we
cannot serve at a distance."

2

Assessing

If you were to ask a group of beginning teachers what kind of help they need from a mentor, many would tell you—as they consistently tell me and other researchers—that they need help with discipline, classroom management, and lesson planning. In addition, most would indicate that they need information about school policies and procedures, that they appreciate timely feedback, and that they hunger for friendly support.

Do all new teachers have the same needs? The answer is yes and no; yes, because there are categories of needs that the majority of new teachers have in common, and no, because there are sets of specific needs within each of these categories that are unique to each individual. You function as an assessor when you gather and analyze data in order to find out what it is that your mentee doesn't know or can't do. You function as an assessor when you identify resources and strategies that will support your mentee's assessed needs. And you function as an assessor when you determine how your mentee will best take in and process information.

Generic Needs of New Teachers

The following exercise will introduce you to some of the generic needs of new teachers. Your mentee will most likely share in a number of them.

Exercise 2.1 *Stuff that make novices nervous*

Below are seven categories that typically contribute to the angst of being a new teacher. I have indicated a situation and an example of a specific need that relates to each category, a need that you can reasonably anticipate your mentee will have. Your task is to add an additional example for each category (you do not need to suggest a solution, although you may, if you wish).

Category: Curriculum (the specific content to be taught in a course)

Situation: The mentee teaches 6th grade science to a class of students from diverse backgrounds and with a variety of developmental abilities.

Example of need: How to select lesson content that is suitable for the level of students' cognitive development and appropriate to their social, emotional, and physical development.

Your situation:

Your example of need:

Category: Instruction (the strategies and methods by which the curriculum is taught)

Situation: Some of your mentee's students learn primarily from visual stimulation, others from auditory stimulation. Most move from one to another with forays into a kinesthetic style.

Example of need: How to teach in ways that will engage the entire range of student learning styles in the class.

Your situation:

Your example of need:

Category: Lesson Planning (mapping out the activities, sequence, use of resources, instructional strategies, and student assessment aspects of a lesson)

Situation: Students in this middle-school mathematics class come into the classroom immediately after lunch. They are usually lethargic and slow to get into the lesson.

Example of need: How to begin a lesson so that students will focus on its content with anticipation.

Your situation:

Your example of need:

Category: Student Assessment (determining the extent to which students understand and can apply the lesson's content)

Situation: Your mentee teaches geography. The students are doing well in her class and they enjoy the subject. She is aware, however, that the students do poorly in the language arts (which she does not teach).

Example of need: How much attention should be paid to spelling and grammar when grading a geography test?

Your situation:

Your example of need:

Category: Classroom Management (making sure that the classroom provides a safe and orderly place in which to learn)

Situation: Your mentee spends an inordinate amount of time distributing and collecting papers and taking care of other classroom routines.

Example of need: How to physically arrange the classroom in order to improve its functionality.

Your situation:

Your example of need:

Category: School Policy (the routines and procedures school personnel are expected to follow)

Situation: Your mentee has arranged a field trip for her students but is uncomfortable about the legal aspects involved.

Example of need: What is involved, and who is responsible for arranging transportation and insurance for a field trip?

Your situation:

Your example of need:

Category: Parents and Community (the nature and degree of involvement, responsibility, and authority parents and community have vis-à-vis the school system)

Situation: Your mentee would like the opportunity to meet his students' parents and guardians.

Example of need: How to get more parents to attend the annual "open house."

Your situation:

Your example of need:

Category: Emotions (the stresses, feelings, and attitudes experienced while carrying out various aspects of the profession)

Situation: Your mentee is scheduled for his first formal evaluation by the Principal. He is really nervous and has asked for your guidance.

Example of need: How to prepare for, cope with, and recover from an evaluation by one's supervisor.

Your situation:

Your example of need:

Specific Needs of Your Mentee

In the above exercise, we listed several examples of categorical concerns that we can assume are shared by many new teachers. But what additional concerns does *your* mentee have?

One way to find out what your mentee needs is to ask him or her. Another way is to keep your eyes and ears open for clues. For example, if you want data about teacher-student interaction, you can go into the classroom and observe these dynamics for yourself. Another source—perhaps the best source of all—from which to get a realistic sense of classroom dynamics is the students themselves.

If you and your mentee are willing to solicit and respect honest student feedback, a process called Small Group Instructional Diagnosis, or SGID, affords the opportunity to gain some insights about classroom dynamics not otherwise obtainable. SGID was pioneered in the 1970s at the University of Washington by Dr. Joseph Clark. It was conceived as a midcourse adjustment strategy and has become a regular feature of hundreds of institutions of higher education throughout the country.

For the following exercise, I have modified the SGID process to make it applicable to middle and high schools. If your mentee is a pre–Kindergarten, Kindergarten, or elementary teacher, I encourage you to experiment with my adaptation and modify SGID even further so that it will resonate more readily with the developmental stage of those younger students.

Exercise 2.2 *Get the students' perspective*

On a prearranged day about halfway through the school year, during the last 30 minutes of the class and in the absence of the first-year teacher, form students into groups of four to six people. You can use cooperative learning groups if they already exist in the class. The reason for using small groups is that they place the extremes of student opinion within the context of group consensus. The procedure also increases validity.

Have each small student group select a recorder, then discuss these three questions: 1) What helps you learn in this class? 2) What gets in the way of your learning, and 3) What can be done to help you learn better? Following 10 minutes of discussion, ask each group to come to consensus on its answers.

Before beginning, make it clear to the students that (a) the discussion will focus on what goes on in the classroom, not on the teacher, and (b) it will be up to the teacher to decide what, if anything, he or she will do about the students' responses.

When all groups have completed their discussions (or when the designated time has expired), have the recorders report their groups' answers to the entire class. Write the comments on the board as they are presented. When all the groups have presented their comments, summarize and clarify until all agree on a class response to each question.

While you are working with the students in the classroom, have your mentee, working alone, ponder the following: 1) What will the students say it is that helps them learn in the class, and what do I (the mentee) think will help? 2) What will the students say it is that gets in the way of their learning, and what do I (the mentee) think it is? and 3) What will the students suggest doing that will improve their ability to learn, and what do I (the mentee) suggest?

The class's small-group discussion is preceded by a pre–SGID conversation and followed by a post–SGID discussion, both of which take place privately between you and your mentee. The pre–SGID meeting provides an opportunity to talk about the purpose of the process and to discuss goals, class activities, and any sensitive aspects or conditions that might apply. The meeting also offers an opportunity to change the generic questions to ones that relate to specific aspects of the class, and to agree on how the information obtained will be treated.

The post–SGID meeting consists of a discussion of the information gathered. The intent is to understand the students' perspectives, to reflect on any differences between student and instructor perceptions, and to decide whether to make any changes based on the activity. The conversation should include a discussion about strategies for any anticipated change and consider what the teacher might say when talking to the students about the SGID's results during the first 5-10 minutes of the next class.

It is important to understand that SGID is not a student evaluation of the teacher. It is a voluntary, confidential assessment process for the mentor-mentee's use only. The information generated by a SGID can be ignored or considered together with other data as an indicator of needs. At the very least, SGID can generate thoughts about possible changes in teaching strategies and/or potential adjustments in a classroom's learning environment. It also offers students a good example of group decision making and consensus building.

Gathering Resources

Another aspect of the assessing function is to identify and have readily available the information and materials that will help your mentee address his or her needs as they arise. In May 1990, the Massachusetts Teachers Association, in collaboration with the Massachusetts Field Center for Teaching and Learning, convened a group of first-year teachers to identify their needs. The conveners published the results of the process along with a series of recommendations in a 23-page report titled "The First Year." The authors of the report observe that "introductions and orientations cannot prepare the beginning teacher for every contingency that will arise in the first year or even the first week." The report goes on to stress that it is essential to provide new teachers with critical information and materials: "To withhold the basic tools needed for success until the new teacher has the time and familiarity with the system to seek them out is to deliberately handicap that person. Imagine not telling the resident surgeon where the operating room is located, or not providing surgical instruments as he/she stands over that first appendectomy."

The following exercise will help you identify and gather material and information that you will want to have available when your mentee needs them.

Exercise 2.3 A treasure hunt for resources

Take another look at the categories in Exercise 2.1. This time, we will
use these categories as a checklist for a treasure hunt. The idea is to
create a file of information that will be useful to your mentee.

Keeping this purpose in mind, search throughout your school,
district, and community for resources that will help address each
category of need. Also, check out the World Wide Web for additional
material. If you do not know where to start looking on the Web, try
http://www.ed.gov (the U.S. Department of Education), http://www.
nea.org (the National Education Association), or http://www.aft.org
(the American Federation of Teachers). Each of these sites provide
links to a wealth of educational materials. To find more Web sites, ask
your local computer guru to tell you about search engines. If you do
not personally have access to the Web, or your school cannot provide
you with access, try your local public library.

Then, in the numbered spaces provided, write the names of one
or two resources that actually exist(s) for each category. Last but not
least, get the resources and file them away for your mentee.

Category: Curriculum

Example of Resource: The results of students' most recent standard-
ized and criterion reference tests.

Another Example: Copies of the National Curriculum Standards for
the mentee's subject area, your state's Curriculum Framework, and
your local district's pertinent Curriculum Guide(s).

1. _____

2. _____

Category: Instruction

Example of Resource: The name of a teacher or teachers in your district who recently completed a series of workshops on instructional
strategies and is willing to share that information.

1. _____

2. _____

Category: Lesson Planning

Example of Resource: Instructions on how to access the regularly updated file of lesson plans available on the Internet through the CompuServe Education Forum.

1. _____

2. _____

Category: Classroom Management

Example of Resource: Suggestions on how to rearrange classroom furniture and equipment to facilitate interactive learning.

1. _____

2. _____

Category: School Policy

Example of Resource: Emergency procedures in case of accident or illness involving students with physical disabilities.

1. _____

2. _____

Category: Parents and Community

Example of Resource: Recent history, policies, and activities of the local Business and School Partnership Program.

1. _____

2. _____

Category: Emotions

Example of Resource: Information regarding the stress management program and other psychological counseling services available at no cost to city employees.

1. _____

2. _____

In addition to the items you identified in Exercise 2.3 above, there are some resources that would be helpful to a new teacher if only they were available. An example of one such potentially valuable resource that is usually nonexistent or hard to find is a tangible collection of insights about the culture and atmosphere of the new teacher's school and community. If your school has a booklet, a videotape, or an annotated scrapbook that portrays the school's unique personality and special qualities, by all means procure and file a copy. If not—or even if it does—the next exercise will prepare you to introduce your mentee to the special qualities of his or her new working environment.

Exercise 2.4 *This is us*

Write a short descriptive piece that describes the mentee's school and community in terms of their special characteristics and qualities, rather than demographics and statistics. Include maps, photographs, and sketches. Complete the following sentences to focus your thoughts.

1. The students in this school . . .
2. Their parents . . .
3. The teachers in this school . . .
4. The nonteaching professional staff, secretaries, and custodians . . .
5. The school's major claim to fame is . . .
6. The first thing that would inspire a stranger upon entering the school is . . .
7. Teaching in this school is like . . .
8. The surrounding community is . . .
9. Some interesting places in town are . . .
10. Local community support for education comes from . . . in the form of . . .

Your Mentee's Learning Preferences

Adults—and children, too, for that matter—have distinct preferences for the way they take in, interact with, and respond to stimuli
in a learning environment.

For example, suppose you want to help your mentee learn to
develop a lesson plan. Would he or she prefer concrete examples or
benefit more from theories and abstractions? Would starting with the
"big picture" be more helpful than supplying step-by-step instructions? Would your mentee rather talk about the process or read about
it? If you are aware of your mentee's particular learning preferences,
you can communicate with him or her more directly than otherwise
by using materials, words, and phrases that will resonate at a deeper
level of understanding.

One way to find out how your mentee prefers to approach a specific learning situation is to ask. Assuming you and your mentee
have an honest and trust-based working relationship, this is an excellent assessment strategy. For example, you could reply to a request
for help planning lessons by saying, "You wanted to talk about developing lesson plans. Do you want to discuss lesson plans in general? Would you like me to critique one of yours? Would you prefer
me to show you how I do it, or do you have some other thoughts or
specific questions?"

Another way to determine learning preferences is to inquire
whether your mentee has recently completed one of the instruments
that have been developed to identify personality and learning styles
and if so, whether he or she would be willing to share its results with
you. Four of the most often administered instruments of this type are:

The Dunn, Dunn, and Price Learning Style Inventory (adult version)
investigates an individual's learning style as influenced by
environmental, emotional, sociological, physical, and psychological elements.

Kolb's Learning Style Inventory organizes responses into two bipolar concepts—concrete experience versus reflective observation, and abstract conceptualism versus active experimentation.
An analysis of responses classifies learners as accommoda-
tors, convergers, assimilators, or divergers.

Gregorc's ORGANON describes the way one perceives images cognitively from concrete to abstract, and suggests that information is ordered either in a sequential fashion or in a random way.

The Myers-Briggs Type Indicator (MBTI) organizes an individual's personality preferences into four bipolar concepts: extroversion versus introversion, sensing versus intuition, thinking versus feeling, and judgment versus perception. The results are used to predict behavior and attitudes.

Although it is generally agreed that one can apply different learning modes in various situations, and that individuals can change their preferred learning style over time, familiarity with your mentee's preferred learning style can suggest how to frame questions and comments and when to propose developmentally paced activities.

Modes of Communication

Suppose your mentee, Frank, says to you, "The kids have been giving me a tough time. I'm planning to rearrange the seating in my classroom: girls on one side and boys on the other." You want to encourage Frank to think about the ramifications of his plan. Which of the following statements would best communicate this to Frank?

1. "I see what you're saying, Frank. But look, will this result in the type of classroom situation you envision?"
2. "I hear what you're saying, Frank. But tell me: Will this result in the type of classroom situation it sounds like you want?"
3. "I'm in touch with your concern, Frank. But help me get a handle on what it is you expect; will this result in the type of classroom situation you hope for?"

The answer is: It depends on Frank's sensory mode at the time.

Our memory banks consist of pictures, words, and feelings. When we communicate with others, both as senders and receivers, we go into these memory banks to search for the pictures, words, or feelings that contain appropriate information. Then we take in or put out that information through our senses—primarily visual, auditory, and feelings (tactile and emotional). We normally do not remain in the same sensory mode throughout an interaction. In fact, most of us develop a particular sequence of sensory modes through which we process various experiences.

When I speak to another person, the words I use usually include sensory predicates such as "see," "hear," "feel," "look," and "listen." If my words are congruent with the particular sensory mode of the listener at the time, I can speed up the whole communication process. The listener does not have to "translate" my information into his or her sensory mode in order to understand.

Neuro-Linguistic Programming (NLP) is a behavioral model that, among other things, suggests that by observing eye movements, a person can quickly determine which of the three modes—visual, auditory, or feeling—another person is using to input, process, and output information. NLP was foreshadowed by Richard Bandler and John Grindler in their book, *The Structure of Magic* (published in 1975 by Science and Behavior Books, Inc., Palo Alto, California), which describes their study of the use and effect of language and nonverbal communication by successful therapists. The concept was further developed in cooperation with Robert Dilts, Leslie C. Bandler, and Judith DeLozier and published in 1980 under the title *Neuro-Linguistic Programming* (see Resource A).

You probably have noticed that during conversations, people will periodically break eye contact and shift their eyes momentarily to another position. NLP postulates that peoples' eyes move off center while accessing some bit of information, and that the direction to which an individual shifts his or her eyes corresponds to the sensory mode being accessed. Dilts et al. contend that generally speaking, when a person's eyes have shifted up and to their right or left, they are accessing internal visual imagery. When a person's eyes move laterally to their right or left, or down to their left, they are accessing internal auditory modes. And when a person is accessing feelings, their eyes will shift down and to their right. For you visually-oriented learners, Figure 2.1 may present a clearer picture.

Although I do not advocate using NLP as a foolproof assessment technique, I do feel comfortable recommending that you learn more about it and consider its use in conjunction with other assessment strategies. At the very least, familiarity with NLP can help you

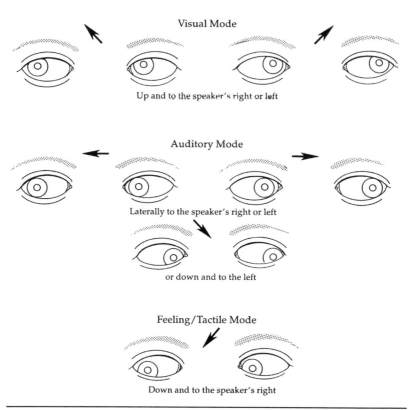

EYE MOVEMENTS AND SENSORY MODES

Visual Mode

Up and to the speaker's right or left

Auditory Mode

Laterally to the speaker's right or left

or down and to the left

Feeling/Tactile Mode

Down and to the speaker's right

Figure 2.1. Neuro-Linguistic Programming (NLP) Eye Movements

understand that your mentee accesses various sensory modes while processing information, and that the way you phrase a statement may communicate more effectively if it resonates with the mode in play at the time.

In summary, you are assessing whenever you take steps to anticipate what your mentee needs in order to grow professionally. Assessing behaviors include

- Taking into consideration the probability that your mentee will experience many of the concerns generic to most beginning teachers—concerns such as those that fall within the categories of curriculum, instruction, lesson planning, classroom management, school policy, interacting with parents and community, and emotions

- Employing a variety of methods to identify your mentee's specific needs—methods such as asking direct questions, observing classroom and other professional performance, and eliciting student perceptions
- Acquiring and developing a variety of resources from a variety of sources to share with your mentee—resources such as those that will help him or her clarify content, determine instructional strategies and activities, acquire and use instructional resources, manage student assessment and classroom environment, understand and follow school policy, work with parents and community, and handle the stresses, feelings, and attitudes experienced while carrying out various aspects of the profession
- Determining your mentee's specific learning preferences— preferences such as those diagnosed by reliable and validated personality and learning style instruments, elicited by directly asking the mentee, and observed by paying attention to shifts in sensory mode and other body language clues

It also important to assess not only what *kind* of mentoring your mentee needs, but also *when* he or she needs it. Chapter 4, Guiding, examines this aspect of the assessing function in detail.

3

Coaching

C oaching: where the rubber meets the road; where it all comes together, baby; where . . . well, you get the idea (feel free to add your own favorite cliché). The point is, coaching is the mentoring function where your relating, assessing, and facilitating behaviors are applied directly to improving your mentee's performance.

Your goal as a coach is to develop your mentee into a self-reliant teacher. By a "self-reliant teacher," I mean a teacher who is willing and able to (a) generate and choose purposefully from among viable alternatives, (b) act upon those choices, (c) monitor and reflect upon the consequences of applying those choices, and (d) modify and adjust in order to enhance student learning.

The athletic coach develops the equivalent of self-reliance in his or her charges by using every opportunity to "raise the bar;" that is, when the athlete can perform at a particular level of ability, the coach sets a higher standard and challenges the athlete to meet it. The mentor of new teachers also coaches by "raising the bar."

As a mentor-coach, your function is to observe your mentee perform and help him or her reach higher standards. Observing and "raising the bar" on your mentee's performance include not only noting and improving classroom behaviors, but also looking at and fine-tuning the problem-solving and decision-making processes taking place before and after that class.

The Preclass Conference

Because you and your mentee will have established and maintained a trusting relationship, it is likely that an opportunity will arise for you to visit one of your mentee's classes. Within a few days prior to the scheduled classroom visit, you and your mentee should meet privately for about 20 to 30 minutes to discuss the upcoming event. Your objective here is to get your mentee to express and clarify learning objectives, fine-tune teaching strategies, anticipate student behaviors, firm up plans for monitoring student learning, and consider ways to adjust instruction.

During this previsit conversation, your function as a mentor-coach is to ask probing questions in ways that will not only encourage your mentee to come up with ideas to enrich the lesson plan, but will also provide him or her with the opportunity to gain confidence as a reflective practitioner. By "reflective practitioner" I mean a teacher who thinks through the consequences of his or her plans and actions and makes modifications based on thoughtful consideration of outcomes. The following example will illustrate this process.

Suppose that you are going to observe Frank, your mentee, teach his high school American History class. You schedule a preobservation conference for the day before your classroom visit. At the start of the conference, you state your objectives—to clarify learning objectives, fine-tune teaching strategies, anticipate student behaviors, firm up plans for monitoring student learning, and consider ways to adjust instruction—and ask Frank whether he has any particular concerns about your classroom visit the next day. You also ask him if there is anything in particular he would like you to pay attention to during your time in the classroom.

Once these issues are addressed, you ask Frank this open-ended question (i.e., a question phrased in a way that elicits information, thoughts and/or feelings, and cannot be answered with merely a yes or no): "What do you expect your students to know and be able to do by the end of the class tomorrow?"

Your reason for asking this question is not only to find out what to expect when you observe the class, but also to provide your mentee with an opportunity to determine for himself whether he is clear about desired student outcomes.

Frank replies, "This lesson is on the ratification of the U.S. Constitution. I expect students to know when the Constitution was ratified and to know why the Federalists were concerned about what the results of the ratification vote would be and what they did to try to sway the vote their way."

Not bad. You could go into Frank's class with an idea of what his learning objectives are. But you are not just a data gatherer here; you are a Mentor in Coaching Mode! What you want now is to get Frank to expand his concept of the lesson's big picture while, at the same time, have him clarify in his own mind exactly what he wants the students to learn, what he will do to facilitate student learning, what materials he will use, what he expects students to do to demonstrate what they have learned, and how he might modify his teaching accordingly. So you ask Frank more questions—you "raise the bar."

Here are some suggestions to help you ask "bar-raising" questions in ways that will achieve your objective:

1. Pick up on a critical word or phrase from your mentee's reply to your previous question and probe for more detail or clarity. For example, Frank mentioned the Federalists and their concern. Your follow-up question can lead Frank to clarify the extent to which he has considered continuity from one lesson to the next, for example, "What have the students learned so far about the Federalists?" The critical word or phrase may also suggest a question that probes for the extent to which Frank has planned a specific teaching strategy, such as "How will you get across to the students the reasons for the Federalists' concern?"

2. Press for specificity. Ask, for example, "What do you want to happen when you . . .?" "What if it happens this way instead?" "What is the sequence of events that will take place within the lesson?" "How would you feel if . . .?" "What has led up to and will follow this lesson?" "What student behaviors do you hope to see or hear?" "How will you know what students have learned and whether they can apply that learning?"

3. Be patient. After asking your question, wait for the answer. There is power in silence; this is when reflection happens.

4. Acknowledge and validate answers by restating them in your own words. Try recognizing feelings in the same way.

5. Avoid using judgmental phrases such as, "Wouldn't it be better to . . . " or "I can't believe you expect that strategy to work." Instead, allow the mentee to be his or her own judge by using phrases

such as, "When you carry out this activity, what student involvement do you hope for?"

6. Resist the temptation to offer advice (there are exceptions, of course. See the section *When to Show and Tell* later in this chapter).

7. Summarize and acknowledge ideas, feelings, and decisions before ending the meeting.

The following exercise provides an opportunity to practice some of these important conferencing skills.

Exercise 3.1 *Asking clarifying questions*

Sarah, your mentee, is a music teacher. During the conference with Sarah prior to visiting her 6th-grade music class, you ask, "Sarah, tell me about your plans for this lesson."

Sarah replies, "I want the students to listen to Mozart, and appreciate his music."

You want Sarah to clarify her objectives, so you ask, "After the lesson is over, what will the students know and be able to do that they couldn't before?"

Sarah thinks for a moment and replies, "My learning objectives are to have students recognize a piece of music as Mozart's and be able to explain how they can tell."

Continuing on with the above conversation, construct a probing, open-ended question relating to each of the lesson components below that will likely cause Sarah to reflect and respond with some specificity.

Instructional activities

Information about materials and how they will be used

Expected student behaviors

Plans to assess student learning

Alternative instructional possibilities

The Classroom Visit

While in your mentee's classroom, you are an objective observer—a human video camera—recording what is going on. Your mentee should be advised ahead of time if you intend to take written notes. Because of the preclass conference, you have a good sense of how the lesson is expected to proceed, so seat yourself in a position to best observe its unfolding.

Be aware that your unfamiliar presence in the classroom, however unobtrusive, will have some influence on what is being observed. When you observe a class, you actually observe a class being observed.

Resist the temptation to become a participant. It is difficult to participate and observe objectively at the same time. Also seductive—and potentially disruptive—is the inclination to envision what you would do if you were teaching the class.

What do you look for in addition to something your mentee may have asked you to observe? If you focus on defects or weaknesses, you are observing your mentee in terms of what is wrong with him or her. Then you find yourself behaving like a pathologist, trying to diagnose symptoms and causes, and hypothesizing remedies. What you really need to be interested in is the extent to which quality learning takes place. Therefore, what you look for first is evidence of student learning, then consider what is contributing to or obstructing the process. Filter all this through the information you derived from the preclass meeting. Now you are ready for the postclass conference.

The Postclass Conference

Your classroom visit has taken place. Prior to observing your mentee in action with students, you met with your mentee to clarify learning objectives, teaching activities, use of materials, expected student behaviors, and plans for monitoring student learning and adjusting instruction. Now, as soon after the observed lesson as possible, you meet again to debrief the event and continue the important coaching function.

Your goal here is to encourage your mentee to assess the effectiveness of the lesson, to identify factors that contributed to and interfered with student learning, and to consider why he or she used alternative instructional strategies at times. Any feedback you give will be in the form of what you saw or heard. Stick to objective facts. Keep your opinions of what went on during the class to yourself. Avoid telling your mentee what you think should have been done.

Your methodology during the postclass conference, as it was during the preclass conference, is to probe with open-ended questions. Here is an example of a series of questions designed to "raise the bar."

How do you think the lesson went?

Why do you think it went the way it did?

How do you know that was the reason?

When you did this . . . the students reacted by. . . . Why do you think that happened?

What did you expect would happen when . . .?

Were there any surprises?

Help me understand what you took into account when planning this particular activity.

I noticed that you altered your prepared lesson plan during (activity X).

If you could teach this lesson again, what, if anything, would you do differently?

Why?

What conclusions can you draw from the way the lesson went?

What conclusions can you draw from our meeting today?

When asking a question to elicit reflection, you need to be careful not to ask in a way that puts down or belittles your mentee. For example, asking your mentee "If you teach this lesson again, don't you think requiring more activity on the part of the students will help them learn better?" implies that he or she didn't plan as well as you would have; the students didn't learn very well so he or she must be a poor teacher; or how could the mentee have overlooked something this obvious? Asking a question embedded with such implied negative overtones speaks more to the emotions than to reason and creates resistance and resentment—hardly an atmosphere conducive to productive reflection. A better way to phrase such a question is, "If you teach this lesson again, will you do anything differently?" or

"When you planned this activity, what expectations did you have for student involvement?" Then you can follow up with, "Do you see any correlation between student involvement in the lesson and the extent of student learning?" The following exercise will help you avoid the use of negative overtones in your questions.

Exercise 3.2 *Avoiding embedded negatives*

Rephrase the following questions to remove any negative overtones.

"Can't you come up with a better way to do that?"

_____

_____

_____

_____

_____

"Why didn't you see that you miscalculated when you planned to have students exchange seats?"

_____

_____

_____

_____

_____

"That probably won't work. Do you have any idea of what you might do instead?"

_____

_____

_____

_____

What you would tell the mentee to do:

_____

_____

_____

Indicator: The teacher keeps students engaged in the activities of the lesson.

Example of Unsuccessful Application: Students who finish an activity early are left to their own devices until the other students are finished.

What you would tell the mentee to do:

_____

_____

_____

Indicator: The teacher effectively manages routines and transitions.

Example of Unsuccessful Application: Ten percent to 15% of class time is usually spent passing out and collecting materials.

What you would tell the mentee to do:

_____

_____

_____

Indicator: The teacher presents appropriate lesson content.

Example of Unsuccessful Application: Student responses and behavior indicate that the teacher uses vocabulary and concepts well above the level of students' cognitive development.

What you would tell the mentee to do:

_____

_____

_____

Indicator: The teacher provides a structure for learning.

Example of Unsuccessful Application: Students seem confused regarding the purpose of the lesson content.

What you would tell the mentee to do:

_____

_____

_____

Indicator: The teacher develops the lesson to promote achievement of the lesson's objectives.

Example of Unsuccessful Application: Although students usually enjoy the activities of a lesson, test results indicate that they are not achieving the lesson's objectives.

What you would tell the mentee to do:

_____

_____

_____

Indicator: The teacher uses appropriate questioning strategies.

Example of Unsuccessful Application: Much of the time, the teacher answers her own questions before the students have time to respond.

What you would tell the mentee to do:

_____

_____

_____

Indicator: The teacher monitors student understanding of the lesson and adjusts instruction when necessary.

Example of Unsuccessful Application: The teacher recognizes that students are misunderstanding or failing to learn, refers to the students as being not very bright, and continues on with the lesson as planned.

What you would tell the mentee to do:

_____

_____

_____

_____

_____

_____

_____

Coaching Adults

Because you are a mentor or are contemplating being one, I can assume that you like a challenge. So how about a little test? True or false: Adults and children have the same orientation to learning.

The answer is false. Adults carry with them a different time perspective and set of experiences from that of children, which in turn produces a difference in the way adults approach learning. An important implication here is that just because someone is a good teacher of children, that doesn't automatically make them a good coach of adults.

The following exercise—a continuation of our little true-false test—will acquaint you with some general characteristics of adult learners. A mentor who understands how an adult takes in and processes information can better coach his or her mentee in ways that communicate directly and clearly.

Exercise 3.4 *How adults learn*

Here are some assumptions about adult learning characteristics. Indicate in each blank whether that statement is true or false.

___ 1. Adults would rather learn something in order to solve a particular problem than learn something just for the sake of learning.

___ 2. Adults will take longer to learn something new than will children.

___ 3. It is easier for adults to learn to do a familiar task in an unfamiliar way than it is to learn a completely new task.

___ 4. When learning something new, adults will take more risks than children.

Here are the answers.

1. True. Adults can't be forced or tricked into learning something new (threats and gold stars notwithstanding). They enter into—even seek out—learning experiences in order to cope with specific life-change events, such as getting and surviving that first teaching job. Adults will engage willingly in learning activities that promise to help them with the transition. To your mentee, learning is a means to an end, not an end in itself.

2. True. The rate of learning increases with age. Learners need to integrate new ideas with what they already know. Incoming data get processed through the filter of experience, and adults have had more experiences than children. Also, information that conflicts with or has little in common with what adults already know is integrated by them more slowly. In contrast with children, adults find that fast-paced, complex learning situations interfere with the integration of new information— especially when the new material forces a reevaluation of what they already know.

3. False. You *can* teach old dogs new tricks; it's teaching them new ways to do old tricks that's the problem. New information that has little relationship to an individual's experience or behavior does not have to be filtered through very much before being added to that person's repertoire. On the other hand, a learner finds it much more difficult to integrate new information into a task that is already familiar. Like most adults, your mentee has acquired a large repertoire of behaviors and

practiced them over a long period of time. Consequently, you need to interact with your mentee with a little more patience and creativity than you might be willing to do with a child.

4. False. As a result of years of experience, adults tend to avoid venturing into trial-and-error territory and opt rather for "safe" assumptions and accurate solutions when mucking around in learning situations. Also, adults tend to let making a mistake affect their self-esteem; therefore they usually stick to the tried and true.

Help Your Mentee Receive Feedback

You can help your mentee get the most out of the pre- and post-class conferences by providing him or her with these guidelines for receiving your feedback:

- Focus on what is being said rather than how it is said.
- Focus on feedback as information rather than as criticism.
- Concentrate on receiving the new information rather than focusing on defending the old.
- Probe for specifics rather than accept generalities.
- Focus on clarifying what has been said by summarizing the main points to the satisfaction of all parties.

In summary, the coaching function's primary objective is to get the mentee to clarify what, when, and how to teach; to reflect on the results of those decisions; and to develop and carry out alternatives that will improve upon past performance.

4

Guiding

Webster's Third New International Dictionary of the English Language, Unabridged defines guide as "vb . . . to direct or supervise esp [sic] toward some desirable end, course, way, or development."

You function as a guide when you systematically direct or supervise your mentee's journey from unseasoned neophyte to self-reliant practitioner. Your purpose as a guide is to bring your mentee to the point where a mentor is no longer necessary, to wean your mentee away from dependence and facilitate his or her journey toward becoming an autonomous teacher.

You establish the groundwork for this journey right from the beginning of your mentor-mentee relationship. When you legitimize and value your mentee's thoughts and feelings, in effect you are taking his or her hand; when you include your mentee in decisions about collecting and assessing data to determine needs, in effect you are gathering resources for the journey; when you ask your mentee to reflect on his or her professional decisions and actions, in effect you are charting the course; and when you encourage your mentee to construct ways to improve his or her teaching, in effect you are opening new avenues to explore.

Guiding Your Mentee's Journey: A Decision-Making Process

Guiding is the mentoring function that is directly concerned with the ongoing professional development of the mentee. In the process of guiding your mentee's professional development journey, you will need to make decisions along the way as to which relating and coaching behaviors will be the most appropriate to use in the various situations you will encounter. These behaviors, or strategies, will not only be those that resonate with the mentee's developmental stage at the time, but will also include those that encourage him or her to strive toward the next-higher level. In order to make such decisions, you need to look at each situation or problem being faced by your mentee in terms of 1) his or her motivation to address it and 2) his or her ability to handle or solve it.

As a general rule of thumb, you decide the *coaching* strategies to use in a given situation based on your assessment of the mentee's level of skills, knowledge, and understanding. You decide the *relating* strategies to use in a given situation based on your assessment of your mentee's level of willingness and motivation and his or her readiness to move on. But first you need to identify and clarify your mentee's situation or problem.

Identifying Your Mentee's Problems

There are several ways to find out what professionally related problems your mentee is facing. For instance, it is safe to assume—as Chapter 2, Assessing, reminds us—that your mentee will share many of the concerns experienced by most beginning teachers.

A direct way to identify a problem specific to your mentee is to go into the classroom and observe its dynamics. Look for clues that tell you what your mentee is doing well, as well as what he or she doesn't know how to do very well. Also look for an indication that your mentee may know something is not going well but is not motivated enough to try to correct the situation.

Suppose, for example, that your mentee is Dorothy. You notice that Cheryl, a student in Dorothy's class, has fallen asleep during a lesson you are observing. After class, you mention the situation to Dorothy, who tells you that Cheryl often dozes off in class and consequently is falling behind academically. Dorothy goes on to say, "Cheryl is not a good student anyhow, and because the other students do not seem to be bothered by her behavior, I'll just let sleeping dogs lie." Obviously, you have identified a problem to work on with Dorothy. It seems that she is not very motivated to do anything about the situation, and chances are that either she does not really understand the need to address it, or she does understand but does not know how to deal with it.

Another way to identify an area of concern is to ask your mentee to reflect on the professional issues he or she is currently experiencing. If there is a difference between the way these issues are unfolding and the way he or she (or you, for that matter) would like them to unfold—and that difference bothers either of you enough to want to do something about it—you probably have identified a significant problem.

Ask your mentee the following questions to stimulate the kind of reflection that can lead to the identification of professional problems or situations that cry out for attention.

What is the most stressful part of your workday? Why?

What recent developments have occurred in your field?

What do you know about your students that helps you teach them more effectively?

Which of your teaching methods is strongest? Weakest?

How would you evaluate whether your students are able to apply what you have taught them to a real-world situation?

In what way did you use supplementary material in a recent class? Why did you use it?

Guiding Principles

Once you have identified and clarified your mentee's problem areas, you are ready to apply these principles:

1. Determine your mentee's motivation and ability to address the problem.
2. Use coaching and relating behaviors that are appropriate to the situation. In general, the less willingness or confidence your mentee exhibits when dealing with a particular situation, the more you need to use relating and reinforcing behaviors. The less knowledge, understanding, and skill your mentee brings to the situation or problem, the more you need to structure your coaching strategies.

3. Use coaching and relating behaviors that "raise the bar," that challenge the mentee to grow professionally.

4. Monitor your mentee's progress, and vary your behaviors accordingly.

The following set of scenarios apply these principles. The vignettes chronicle four events involving James, a beginning teacher, that take place during his first year. Each episode finds James in a different situation, and each situation requires a different kind of mentoring behavior—a different kind of guidance.

The Unwilling and Unable Mentee

It is the beginning of a school year and you are mentoring James, a first-year teacher. James has passed the state university's rigid and comprehensive teacher preparation program and clearly knows his subject matter. He is a bright young man, but a bit shy. You ask to observe one of his classes during the second week of school. James agrees, but reluctantly.

During your visit to his classroom, it is evident that James is having difficulty managing student discipline. His attempts to entice and inveigle students into behaving have little success.

After class, James says to you, "Did you see Jimmy throw that paper clip?"

You nod.

His gaze shifts toward the floor. "I wish the other students hadn't made such a big deal about it."

You note that James's eyes lowered to his right and that he used the words, "I wish." Because both of these reactions are clues that he is in a feeling sensory mode, you ask:

"You feel as though the students are being disruptive?"

"Yes. Their acting out is interfering with my teaching. I'm not sure that I can turn things around. I've tried. It's very discouraging."

Your assessment of James's classroom discipline problem indicates that he needs help on two levels: He needs the skills to solve the problem and the willingness and confidence to tackle it. What do you do?

Coaching Strategies

The immediacy of this situation and James's obvious need for structure call for a "show-and-tell" style of coaching. "This is what to do, James," you tell him. "Rearrange seating [show him how]; establish and maintain rules and standards of behavior [give him a list]; avoid using sarcasm; don't plead for attention; show enthusiasm for the content and for learning; and announce and apply consequences for inappropriate student behavior [give him a list of such consequences]." You are encouraged when James looks at your list of punishments for students not following rules and asks, "Shouldn't there be positive consequences for appropriate behavior?"

Invite James to observe one of your classes to see how you manage discipline. If appropriate, arrange for him to observe another teacher's techniques.

Relating Strategies

You will need to strengthen and support James's willingness and motivation to apply your suggestions. You cannot "motivate" someone else. Motivation is self-constructed. The extent to which a mentee is willing to take some action is influenced by what he or she perceives as important and by what he or she believes can be accomplished. The more a situation affects one's values and the higher one's expectations of success, the stronger the motivation.

Given James's seeming lack of motivation to work out his own classroom management problem, you should 1) increase expectations of success, and 2) encourage his sense of responsibility. These strategies are especially important because they are germane to helping James become a self-reliant teacher.

Here are some specific ways to support James and enhance his self-confidence.

Set short-term, realistic goals; for example, tell James to try out the techniques you shared with him for the next 3 days, after which you will meet to discuss what happened and what to do next.

Acknowledge James's efforts and validate his ideas. Be honest and specific. For example, tell him that he showed insight when he suggested adding rewards for "appropriate" behavior to your list of consequences for inappropriate behavior.

You can also support James by defusing any unjust criticism and by providing resources that will help him carry out the new strategies.

In general, when your mentee is both unmotivated and unable to deal with a situation, your coaching and relating strategies should focus on behaviors that will "fix" that particular problem. However, soon thereafter, it is important to switch to a reflecting style of coaching and place responsibility once again on the mentee.

The Moderately Willing and Somewhat Able Mentee

It is a week later, and James is working hard on his class management problem. It is still not quite under control, but there are signs of improvement. At the end of a conversation about the situation, James says to you, "I've been thinking of changing the way I had planned to teach a particular unit in October, but I'm uncertain about some of the details. Can we discuss my ideas?"

You are elated. By the nature of his statement, James has indicated his readiness and willingness to approach *this* situation by sharing ideas and exploring new strategies together. In other words, your assessment of James's sense of competency and confidence in this instance suggests that he would prefer to work in collaboration with his mentor and contribute to discussions—clearly a different level of ability and motivation from what he exhibited in the discipline scenario. James's words and attitude show that he is willing to take responsibility for clarifying concepts about teaching and learning and to share in the making of informed decisions. What do you do?

Coaching Strategies

Your strategy in this situation is to encourage James to reflect on his ideas. Ask him probing, open-ended questions, such as, "How do you see this new activity engaging students more powerfully than the one you had planned to use?" or "What research or precedents support this new strategy?" This is also an opportunity for you both to brainstorm for alternative strategies and to discuss possible resources.

When you and James have agreed on a particular new approach, encourage him to try it out and see what happens. Offer to observe that class—or suggest that James have the class videotaped—and to meet with him afterward to discuss and fine-tune the outcome. During that postclass meeting, you might say something like, "We both agree that the new activity went well and that most of the students grasped the concept rather quickly. I noticed, however, that the new activity left some of the students so stimulated that it took them a long time to get into the next activity. Let's brainstorm ways that might have helped those students settle down more quickly. Will you have time during the week to see what the literature has to offer in the way of suggestions?"

Your follow-up strategy is to continue to encourage and help James find and use resources, human and otherwise; make informed decisions; take some considered risks; and reflect on the outcomes of those actions.

As James becomes more competent, you gradually offer less direction and cooperation and begin to encourage James to try out and evaluate his own ideas, letting him know that you are interested in hearing about them and how they are working.

Relating Strategies

Listen to James's ideas. Let him know you are paying attention. Do this through the use of body language and by paraphrasing back to him what you understood him to have said.

Celebrate James's successes by sending his principal or supervisor a note (copied to James) commending James's initiative and citing any resultant improvement in student learning.

Let James know that you appreciated having been asked to discuss his ideas. Offer to look over and provide feedback on other ideas he might have.

Give James an opportunity for some guided practice by offering to help him revise curriculum or other lesson plans.

The Competent and Confident Mentee

It is the first day back from spring vacation. You pass James in the hall, return his smile, and nod your greetings to each other. What a change from the beginning of the school year when James was having so much trouble with student discipline! Now, when it comes to maintaining a productive classroom climate, James is a master. He is sensitive to subtle shifts in student attention, is able to orchestrate and focus student participation, and has the flexibility to recognize and take advantage of teachable moments. As a mentor, what do you do?

Coaching and Relating Strategies

Honor James's strength in this area by not interfering. You might let him know that you recognize his success. Suggest that he outline his strategies so that he can share his techniques with his colleagues in some way, perhaps by presenting a workshop or leading an informal discussion around the topic.

The "All-of-the-Above" Mentee

Chances are that your mentee will be at different stages of ability and motivation in various teaching scenarios. As we have just seen, for example, James has acquired a great deal of competence and confidence in establishing rapport with students. He is also adept at maintaining an effective classroom climate. Obviously, he now needs very little mentoring in this area.

In another regard, James tells you that he is pleased with the way his lesson-planning ability has improved since the beginning of the year. He also lets you know that he has taken up the challenge of continuing to improve in that area. Your appropriate mentoring style now is to provide collaboration and encouragement rather than offering specific suggestions or adopting a "noninvolvement" attitude.

Exercise 4.1 *Help James assess his students*

Suppose you notice, however, that James often takes it for granted that students understand more than they actually do. As a result, he gets frustrated and discouraged when student test results fail to support his estimation of the students' understanding. What would you do? What relating and coaching behaviors are appropriate? Write your ideas below.

_____

_____

_____

_____

Discussion: You could have written a variety of appropriate behaviors. In general, structured coaching strategies and objective, non-judgmental listening behaviors are called for here. Coaching behaviors that respond to James's need to clarify and restructure his student assessment efforts are appropriate. He also needs from you relating behaviors that will help him resolve the emotional issues connected with the pedagogical ones. Do the strategies you listed satisfy these requirements?

In the above scenarios, we see that a mentee can exhibit the need for different mentoring strategies in different situations at relatively the same time. You are a successful mentor in these scenarios not only because you exhibit good coaching, relating, and guiding skills, but also because you assess and diagnose effectively, you are flexible, and you are able to use appropriate behaviors in a variety of given situations.

_____

Exercise 4.2 *Practice choosing the appropriate behavior*

In this exercise, you will have the opportunity to practice your diagnostic skills. For each situation below, there are four alternative behaviors. Decide on the most appropriate behavior for that situation.

Situation 1: You and your mentee, Lois, have been getting along well; in fact, you have become good friends. Professionally, you have recently switched from a structured to a looser reflecting style of coaching to help Lois improve her ability to develop lesson plans. You started originally with a "show-and-tell" style because Lois exhibited few lesson-planning skills at the time. Progress has been slow but steady. Recently, however, Lois's interest in improving has waned, and her lesson-planning ability has regressed back to the point where it is almost nonexistent. You would:

   a. Switch back to "show-and-tell" coaching

   b. Discuss the situation with Lois and mutually agree on a solution

   c. Continue using a reflective style but let Lois know you are concerned

   d. Remain friendly on a personal level, but adopt a "hands-off" posture professionally

Discussion: The most appropriate immediate behavior is a. You need to get Lois back on track in a hurry. When she begins to show signs of willingness to resume some responsibility, you can let up a bit and go to a more collaborative style such as b. Alternative c holds little promise until motivation increases. Alternative d will only make the situation worse, because Lois does not have the skills to improve on her own.

Situation 2: Your and your mentee, Sam, have worked together to establish an effective and supportive classroom climate. Your successful coaching behavior was to ask probing questions that encouraged Sam to reflect and to construct his own classroom strategies. Until recently, Sam has experienced no major discipline problem. However, a student has begun to act out and Sam has been unable to control the boy's continuous disruptive behavior. Sam asks you for help. You would

   a. Go into Sam's classroom and deal with the disruptive student yourself

   b. Encourage Sam to work out a solution himself

   c. Brainstorm some ideas with Sam, let him try some out, and meet later to reflect on their effectiveness

   d. Listen to Sam's ideas about how to solve the problem and give him feedback

Discussion: The most appropriate behavior is c. Sam has shown the willingness and ability to work on classroom discipline with you in the past, and for the most part has been able to do so successfully on his own since then. However, he has asked for your help in this instance. You can best help by revisiting with him the behaviors that worked before. Alternative a is not only an overreaction; it also undermines Sam's rapport with his class. Alternatives b and d are inappropriate because Sam has already tried and been unsuccessful; he does need some help and is wise enough to ask. Once the problem is solved, you no longer need to be involved.

Situation 3: You are an experienced physical education teacher in a small school district. A new state mandate requires a change in the physical education curriculum. Jane was hired this year as the district's only other physical education teacher. You are Jane's mentor. Since the opening day of the school year, Jane has handled responsibility extremely well. She also has exhibited an excellent understanding of her subject and how to teach it. Jane agrees with the state mandate and respects the need for curriculum revision. Although she has no previous experience with curriculum revision, Jane is very good at tracking down information when she needs to. You would

    a. Oversee the curriculum revision, but allow Jane considerable involvement and input

    b. Delegate to Jane the authority and responsibility for the revision

    c. Revise the curriculum yourself and make sure Jane understands and follows it

    d. Revise the curriculum, but ask for Jane's recommendations

Discussion: The most appropriate behavior is b. Jane is knowledgeable and highly motivated in regard to this situation and needs little intervention from you other than some resources, proofreading, and perhaps a little help with formatting a curriculum document. Because the revised curriculum will be "her baby," Jane will be very likely to follow it, reflect on its implementation, and upgrade it as needed. Delegating this responsibility to Jane not only will validate her professionalism, it will also move her toward becoming even more self-reliant. Alternative a would be the appropriate choice if you have legitimate doubts about Jane's ability in the area of curriculum development and feel that she needs direction in this regard. Alternative d does not take full advantage of—nor does it honor— Jane's potential. Alternative c not only ignores Jane's competence and confidence, it also undermines the mentor-mentee relationship by eroding trust.

Situation 4: As a first-year teacher, Michael, your mentee, is doing well in the classroom. Recently, however, he has become a nonconformist when it comes to following school policy and paying attention to everyday procedures. Some of the staff and other teachers are getting annoyed with Michael because they perceive that his behavior will soon be causing problems. When you point this situation out to Michael, he tells you that he will try to pay more attention to policies and procedures, but after a week or two, there is no change. You would

   a. Keep a low profile, allow Michael to experience the consequences of his behavior, and let him take responsibility for working out his own problems

   b. Insist that Michael follow the rules and keep close tabs on his behavior

   c. Ask Michael how he will deal with the situation and offer your help and advice

   d. Redefine and clarify for Michael the expectations and responsibilities having to do with policies and procedures, monitor his progress, and reinforce positive behavior

Discussion: The most appropriate behavior is d. Michael needs to understand and appreciate the rationale behind the school's policies and procedures and take responsibility for adhering to them. This situation initially calls for a structured rather than reflective coaching behavior, coupled with an attentive and supportive relationship style. Alternative a will only increase the probability that the behavior will continue, and possibly worsen. Alternative b is too drastic in that it ignores the need for increased motivation and will probably have an adverse effect on the mentor-mentee relationship as well. Alternative c asks the unmotivated mentee to make an uninformed decision.

Situation 5: Alejandro, your mentee, tells you that he is uncomfortable with the way he had planned to teach the "cells and genes" unit of his general biology class. He has a few ideas about how he might approach the unit differently and has asked you to help him decide which one to use. You would:

a. Hear Alejandro's ideas, tell him which one seems to have the most merit, and thank him for asking for your help

b. Get Alejandro to reflect on his alternative ideas, perhaps generate new ones together, agree on the one to try, and arrange to discuss the results

c. Ask Alejandro to describe his original plan, listen attentively to his alternate ideas, validate his feelings, then encourage him to decide for himself which idea to use

d. Listen to what Alejandro has to say, then share with him a solution that works for you in such a situation and suggest he use it too

Discussion: Alternatives a, b, and c each pay attention to the relationship, but it is behavior b that responds best to Alejandro's readiness for a collaborative style of coaching. Alternative a takes care of Alejandro's request to help him make up his mind, but misses the opportunity to help him develop his problem-solving skills. Alternative c ignores the probability that Alejandro's competence is not yet strong enough to support a confident decision. Alternative d disregards Alejandro's readiness for collaboration.

From Mentor-Mentee to Peer-Peer

The purpose of the guiding function is to wean your mentee away from relying on you for direction and suggestions. The goal is to make your role as mentor no longer necessary. You will know you have achieved this goal when your mentee demonstrates the willingness and ability to make informed professional decisions autonomously; to act on those decisions with confidence; to reflect on the effectiveness of those actions; and to modify procedures based on thoughtful analysis of accurate data. At this point—usually by the end of the first through the middle of the second year of teaching—the status of your collegial relationship will have transformed from mentor-mentee to peer-peer, a partnership in which you each function as a mentor for the other.

I would like to end this chapter with a suggestion. When your former mentee has become a self-reliant teacher, give him or her this advice: Do as I did, BECOME A MENTOR TO A NEW TEACHER!

Tips and Observations

Set Ground Rules Early

At the beginning of your association with a mentee, discuss the objectives of the relationship. Sort out roles, boundaries, expectations, and processes. If there is disagreement, or if you do not know the answer to a question, present your position and feelings honestly so that there will be no false assumptions.

Help Change Happen

If you are thwarted in attempts to bring about a change in your mentee or in the mentoring process, try the following:

1. Define the desired change using specific, measurable terms.
2. List everything you can think of that is resisting or getting in the way of that change.
3. List everything you can think of that is helping or can help that change take place.
4. Develop strategies to intensify items that help, dilute items that hinder, and change resisting items into supporting ones.

Avoid Information Overload

Provide information and material to your mentee as needed. Don't saturate him or her with particulars months, weeks, or even days before there is a need to know; the minutiae will get filtered out in favor of more immediate needs. For example, delay a discussion of parent-teacher meeting protocol until shortly before any meetings are scheduled to take place.

Share Decision Making

When you have identified a mentee's need, don't assume that he or she agrees with you. Work together on identifying needs. Reach an agreement concerning what to work on.

Know When to Intervene

Know when to step in and when to stand back from a touchy situation. Intervene when a situation threatens someone's health and safety. Intervene if your mentee has failed in several attempts to handle a problem and specifically asks for your intervention. Avoid intervening when doing so will detract from your mentee's credibility. Consider whether intervening will keep your mentee from an opportunity to learn and grow.

Mentoring, Remediating, and Peer Review

You may be called upon to work with, or mentor, another veteran teacher, one whose performance has been evaluated as being below par. Much of the material in this book can apply in such a situation. However, if you are expected to *remediate* the "mentee," mentoring is not what will be going on. Being mentored means you are developing the capacity to fix yourself; being remediated means someone else is fixing you. In addition, if you are expected to *evaluate* the other teacher, the vital element of trust so necessary in a mentor-mentee relationship is likely to be compromised. In this situation, your focus should not be on peer review, but on peer assistance; not on assessing your colleague's competency, but rather on helping the teacher prepare for assessment by someone else.

Suppose you are asked to submit a written report on your mentee's progress. You can honor that request, but in that report, you want to make it clear—either directly or through implication—that your role as a mentor precludes you from formally evaluating your mentee. You should share the report with your mentee, not only for his or her information, but also in order to reinforce the trust and confidentiality of the mentor-mentee relationship. For example, a phrase you might use in such a report is, "My role as mentor is to facilitate _____'s efforts to determine and address his own professional development needs. We are involved in this process and it is progressing well."

Maintain the Relationship

Where personalities and schedules permit, employ a medley of relationship-building opportunities with your mentee. Attend workshops and meetings together, for example. Engage in informal chitchat about teaching, politics, sports, or books—perhaps over coffee or lunch, or while jogging or playing golf. All too often, mentors and mentees tend to decrease their contact under the press of other demands.

Don't Forget Content

Take every opportunity to keep your mentee up to speed on the subject he or she teaches. Encourage membership and participation in professional associations. Get your school's professional library to subscribe to relevant periodicals and acquire pertinent publications. Share and discuss the most recent national, state, and local curriculum standards. Review together and discuss the potential use of newly available texts and supplementary material. Also, you should check to see whether your state is one of the 33 that are members of the Interstate New Teacher Assessment and Support Consortium. INTASC is a program of the Council of Chief State School Officers and is concerned with teacher licensing procedures. Because INTASC is working on developing content-specific standards that will be used for assessing beginning teachers, you will want to be sure that your mentee knows of and can meet those standards. INTASC has already designed prototype assessment standards based on English, language arts, and mathematics. Others are being considered.

Know When to Wean

"Enough, already!" This is what Ms. Greene, a department chair, had to tell a mentor. The mentor had done a good job mentoring a teacher in Ms. Greene's department, but had long since passed the point where the mentee needed a mentor. The relationship had become a parent-child one. Don't become a "professional mentor." Know when to let go.

Find Time to Mentor

With luck, you and your mentee will be able to arrange 10 to 15 minutes together before and after school, during lunch or free periods, between sessions at conferences or meetings, and even during bus or cafeteria duty. Although a lot can be discussed and accomplished in short periods if you focus, this is really not enough time to analyze, plan, and create.

Yes, arranging longer blocks of time can present difficulties. But if mentoring is a high enough priority, you will find some way to create the time. Mentoring activities that require about 30 minutes include classroom observations, the SGID process discussed in chapter 2, and associated pre- and postclass conferences. Ideally, those who plan and administer mentoring programs will have arranged the time for you and your mentee to work together. Your district may even have been the recipient of a grant to "buy" the time in the form of stipends, substitutes, or creative scheduling configurations. If not—or even if they have—here are a couple of things *you* can do.

Videotape your mentee's class. You will still need face-to-face pre- and postclass conferences, but they can be scheduled more flexibly than classroom visits. You can then review the tape at your convenience, and use it during the postclass conference.

Another way to free up a block of time during the school day is to make the following type of arrangement with a colleague. Together, develop a schedule for the year that combines both classes at regular intervals—say, once every other week. Alternate teaching the combined class. Because you will know well ahead of time when your class size will double, you can plan lessons accordingly. Be sure to get your principal's permission and cooperation.

Earn Points Toward
Teacher Recertification

Several state Departments of Education require certified teachers to periodically renew their teaching credentials. Typically, teachers meet this mandate by earning a minimum number of Continuing Education Units (CEUs), Professional Development Points (PDPs), or some other indicator of time spent participating in professional development activities. Generally, documented independent study can also earn credit toward recertification.

If your state has such a mandate and you are mentoring or preparing to mentor a colleague, you may be able to apply the time you are engaged in completing the exercises in this book toward fulfilling your teaching recertification requirement. Check with the person in your school district responsible for professional development, personnel, or human resources to determine whether your state and local policies allow focused independent study, such as this book's format provides, to earn recertification points. Working through all of this book's exercises should take about 10 to 12 hours.

Reflect on Your Mentoring

Keep an ongoing journal of your mentoring experience. I suggest a three-column format. Record what you did, indicate why you did it, and report what resulted. Include impressions, feelings, and anecdotes. Reflect on your journal entries and note, for example, how you might approach a particular situation differently next time. You might want to share some of your entries with your mentee. Encourage your mentee to keep a similar journal.

Consider Multiple Mentors

It may be advantageous to share your mentee with another mentor. The option allows you to devote less time to the mentee and to discuss confidential issues concerning the mentee with a colleague.

Build a Mentoring Community

In his article, "Preparing Mentors of Beginning Teachers: An Overview for Staff Developers" (Journal of Staff Development, Vol. 17, No. 4), Tom Ganser warns, " . . . designating individuals as 'official' mentors can cause other teachers, administrators, and school personnel to abdicate their professional obligation toward the beginning teacher. They may inaccurately look upon the mentor as the only person responsible for assisting the beginner rather than being an integral part of a complex process that includes them as well."

Sharon Daloz Parks, Associate Professor of Pastoral Theology and Human Development at Weston School of Theology, expanded on Ganser's admonition during a plenary address given in San Francisco at the 1990 annual meeting of the American Association of Higher Education. Parks contends, "A single mentor is sufficient for an initiation into the conventions of the corporation or the university or the society as each is presently constituted. But if one is to be initiated into a . . . more adequate . . . alternative . . ., nothing less than a mentoring community will do." She goes on to say that "[o]ngoing research makes it increasingly evident that those who are able to work on behalf of personal and social transformation are those who . . . were part of a mentoring community—a group who shared a . . . mentoring vision."

Find Networking Opportunities

If you are the only mentor, or have only one or two mentoring colleagues in your district, it is desirable that you have a support system so that you are not operating in isolation. All educators, even mentors, need inspiration and encouragement to continue to learn and grow professionally. In case your local or neighboring educational community does not provide the opportunity to interact periodically with other mentors, some professional associations offer this service. The Association for Supervision and Curriculum Development (ASCD), for example, supports a Mentoring Leadership and Resources Network. Several virtual networking communities are available to mentors. If you have access to the Internet and the World Wide Web, conduct a search for on-line education support groups. Using "mentoring" as a key search word will uncover many interesting sites. I do not specify any of these sites here because the mix constantly changes as older ones atrophy and new ones are formed.

Remember, Student Learning Is the Goal

Always keep in mind that the ultimate purpose behind your efforts to improve your mentee's teaching is to improve student learning. When assessing your mentee's needs, ask yourself: "What else does this beginning teacher need to know and be able to do in order to help students achieve what they need to know and be able to do?"

How to Contact the Author

Please feel free to contact me (Hal Portner) with feedback, suggestions, questions, or anecdotes about your mentoring experiences, or just to say "hello." I can be reached by e-mail:

portner_associates@compuserve.com

or by fax at (413) 586-4190.

Resource A: Annotated Bibliography

The publications I have chosen to include in this bibliography are those that illustrate and expand upon the research and models behind the behaviors discussed in this book—the functional behaviors associated with mentoring new teachers. This is not a survey of writings about the history and philosophy of mentoring, nor does it make much reference to publications concerned with planning and implementing mentoring programs. I have made this an annotated bibliography rather than simply a list of references because I want to entice you, the reader, to inquire further into various aspects of mentoring behavior. Although this is not an exhaustive survey of the extant literature, it does provide enough of a panoramic view of what is available should you want to increase your knowledge base and sharpen your mentoring effectiveness.

Brookfield, S. D. (1995). *Becoming a critically reflective teacher.* San Francisco: Jossey-Bass.

Applying the principles of adult learning, Brookfield tells teachers how they can reframe their teaching by examining their practices from the perspectives of their own experiences as teachers and learners, the perceptions of their students and colleagues, and the lessons of theory. Throughout the book, he describes strategies and practical approaches to critical reflection, including the use of teaching diaries, role-model portfolios, participant-learning portfolios, structured critical conversation, and the Good Practices Audit—a process in which teachers search their experiences for good responses to common problems they encounter. Brookfield devotes a chapter to negotiating the risks and apparent contradictions of critical reflection and ends his book with an argument for the creation of a culture of reflection.

Carkhuff, R. R. (1993). *The art of helping* (7th ed.). Amherst, MA: Human Resource Development Press.

Robert Carkhuff's helping process begins with what he calls "the most profound step: relating interpersonally," and culminates with ". . . empowering people to actualize their own human potential." The seventh edition discusses the helping process in terms of the helpee's and helper's contribution to the process. The author also describes and provides examples of four helping skills—attending, responding, personalizing, and initiating—to which the main body of his book is devoted. A comprehensive list of "feeling words" appears in the appendix.

Claxton, C. S., & Murrell, P. H. (1987). *Learning styles: Implications for improving education practices.* ASHE-ERIC Higher Education Report No. 4. Washington, DC: Association for the Study of Higher Education.

Claxton and Murrell examine various approaches to understanding how people learn and classify these approaches in terms of personality, information processing, social interaction, and instructional methods. The authors then describe models that have been developed in each of the four classifications and discuss their potential applications.

Personality models discussed include Herman A. Witkin's Field Dependence-Independence Dimension of Cognitive Style, which determines the extent to which a person is influenced by the surroundings and the ramifications of that degree of influence; the Myers-Briggs Type Indicator (MBTI), which considers the ways in which people take in information and how they choose to make decisions; the Reflection Versus Impulsivity model, which contrasts the tendency to reflect over alternative solution possibilities with the tendency to select impulsively; the Omnibus Personality Inventory (OPI), which measures long-term intellectual, interpersonal, and social-emotional development; and the Holland Typology of Personality, which posits six personality types: Realistic, Investigative, Social, Conventional, Enterprising, and Artistic.

Information-processing models discussed are those by Gordon Pask, which looks at the way people approach learning in terms of holistic vs. serialistic strategies; by Siegle and Siegle, which describes a continuum ranging from factual to conceptual learning preferences; by R. Schmeck, which classifies information processors by devoting more attention to the meaning and classification of an idea suggested by a symbol rather than to the symbol itself; by David Kolb, termed "experiential learning," which describes learning as a four-step cyclic process incorporating concrete experience, reflective observation, abstract conceptualization, and active experimentation; and by Anthony Gregorc, which postulates that learning occurs both through concrete experience and abstraction, either randomly or sequentially.

Social-interaction models were developed by Mann et al., which categorizes learners into eight behavioral clusters: compliant, anxious-dependent, discouraged workers, independent, heroes, snipers, attention seekers, and silent; by Grasha and Reichmann, which classifies learners as independent, dependent, collaborative, competitive, participant or avoidant; by Fuhrmann and Jacobs, which involves dependent, collaborative, and independent styles; and by Eison, which identifies style in terms of attitude toward grading and learning.

Instructional-preference models discussed are by Joseph Hill, which maps and interprets the learning style preferred by the learner, such as symbols, culture, influence, memory, cognition, teaching style, and decision making; and by Albert Canfield, which is concerned with conditions of learning (affiliation, structure, achievement, and eminence) and the content of learning (numerics and logic, language, things, and people).

The authors suggest that by understanding our own and others' learning preferences, we can become, and help others become, more active participants in the learning process.

Colton, A. B., & Sparks-Langer, G. M. (1993). A conceptual framework to guide the development of teacher reflection and decision making. *Journal of Teacher Education, 44*(1), 45-54.

The authors have developed what they term "a conceptual framework that portrays the mental processes [of teachers who are] reflective decision makers." As part of the process of reflective decision making, Colton and Sparks-Langer see teachers considering the immediate and long-term social and ethical implications of their decisions.

The article touches on cognitive psychology, critical theory, and the theories of motivation and caring, the background theories upon which the framework is based. It then presents the framework itself, which integrates cognitive, critical, and personal characteristics. The authors identify seven categories of knowledge in a reflective teacher: content, students, pedagogy, context, prior experiences, personal views and values, and scripts. The framework also identifies three categories of action re-lating to decisions: planning, implementation, and evaluation. The authors contend that knowledge and meaning are constructed as teach-ers interpret reality in light of their professional knowledge base; that feelings have an influence on the ability to reflect; and that efficacy, flexibility, social responsibility, and consciousness supported by a col-legial environment drive and support teacher reflection.

Costa, A., Garmston, R., Zimmerman, D., & D'Arcangelo, M. (1988). *Another set of eyes: Conferencing skills, trainer's manual.* Alexandria, VA: Association for Supervision and Curriculum Development.

The authors present and discuss the techniques needed for effective cog-nitive coaching. Included are the conferencing skills of questioning, lis-tening, paraphrasing, and probing for specificity. Activities that pro-vide opportunities for practice are provided and a supplementary videotape is available.

Dilts, R., Grinder, J., Bandler, R., Bandler, L. C., & DeLozier, J. (1980). *Neuro-linguistic programming: Volume 1, The study of the structure of subjective experience.* Cupertino, CA: Meta.

In the early 1970s, Richard Bandler and John Grinder, by virtue of collecting and analyzing the communication styles and structures of successful psychotherapists, found themselves in possession of what they saw as a set of powerful and effective communication models. This book generalizes these models for use in other areas of human commu-nication—specifically, business, law, and education.

The introduction and several chapters of the book describe in detail the structure and system of Neuro-Linguistic Programming (NLP), the mechanics and implications of its strategies, the form and content of its utilization in various settings, and rules of thumb in designing and redesigning its form.

Chapter III, Elicitation, and Chapter IV, Utilization, are the two chap-ters most applicable to mentoring new teachers. Chapter III not only goes into detail about eye movements as assessing cues to sensory mo-dalities; it also describes the assessing cues of gestures, breathing, pos-ture, muscle tone, vocal tone, and tempo of speech. Chapter IV intro-duces pacing. Briefly, pacing is the process of feeding back to another person, through your own behavior, the behaviors and strategies that you have observed in them—that is, going into their model of the world and becoming synchronized with their own internal process—thereby building rapport and trust.

Fast, J. (1970). *Body language.* New York: M. Evans.

Kinesics, as the author calls the study of body language, is based on the behavioral patterns of nonverbal communication. It can include any nonreflexive or reflexive movement of a part, or all, of the body, used by a person to communicate an emotional message to the outside world. Using a number of anecdotes and examples, Fast shows how both the delivery and reception of body language can greatly enhance and enrich verbal communication. He also warns that the cultural nuances of body language can lead to misinterpretation.

Included in Fast's survey of the topic are considerations of such aspects of body language as social and public space; facial expressions; touch; posture; eye contact; the movement and positioning of arms, legs and hands; and how people—often unconsciously—may contradict as well as support their words with their behavior.

Hartzel, G. N. (1990). Induction of experienced teachers into a new school site. *Journal of Staff Development, 11*(4), 28-31.

This article from the National Staff Development Council's informative journal highlights differences between novice teachers and experienced newcomers, and suggests six areas that principals (and I would add mentors) need to address with experienced teachers who are new to the school: (1) a realistic view of the school, (2) the emotional aspects involved in the transition, (3) the informal socialization process, (4) appropriate reallocation of tasks, (5) involvement in important tasks, and (6) the provision of regular feedback.

Hiemstra, R., & Brockett, R. G. (Eds.). (1994). Overcoming resistance to self-direction in adult learning. In R. G. Brockett & A. B. Knox (Eds.), *New directions for adult and continuing education,* No. 64. San Francisco: Jossey-Bass.

One of the tasks of a mentor is to help mentees take increasing responsibility for their own learning. The intent of this publication is to help its readers understand some of the sources of resistance to self-directed learning and to identify strategies to overcome such resistance. The 11 chapters are written by people who are carrying out research related to self-direction in learning in a variety of settings. They explore myths that contribute to resistance; discuss key terms, strategies, and techniques for overcoming resistance; examine the literature related to the topic; propose portfolio assessment as a particular strategy; describe how self-directed learning has been used in continuing education by various professional groups, including physicians and architects, and for career advancement by power utility employees; describe how technology and psychometric instruments have been used to enhance and measure individualized learning; and suggest several aspects of the learning process over which learners can assume some control.

Kolb, D. A. (1984). *Experiential learning.* Englewood Cliffs, NJ: Prentice Hall.

Kolb builds on the concept of experiential learning as it emerged in the works of Dewey, Lewin, and Piaget and analyzes its contemporary applications in education, organization development, management development, and adult development. Of special interest to mentors are Chapters 4—"Individuality in Learning and the Concept of Learning Styles"—and 7—"Learning and Development in Higher Education." Kolb's Learning Style Indicator is described and discussed at length in Chapter 4, and the consequences of matches and mismatches between learning style and teaching styles in Chapter 7.

Lee, G. V., & Barnett, B. G. (1994). Using reflective questioning to promote collaborative dialogue. *Journal of Staff Development, 15*(1), 16-21.

Lee and Barnett contend that reflective questioning—a technique in which one person prepares and asks questions that are designed to provide opportunities for the respondent to explore his or her knowledge, skills, experiences, attitudes, beliefs, and values—is a skill that can be developed and used by educators with peers, clients, supervisors, students, and mentees.

This article, based on the authors' experiences teaching the skill, includes information about the origin of the strategy, describes various forms of reflective questioning, delineates conditions that support its use, and provides guidelines for formulating and asking reflective questions.

Manthei, J. (1990). *Mentor teacher preparation inventory and guide for planning and action.* Boston: The Massachusetts Field Center for Teaching and Learning.

This is a self-assessment instrument for teachers who plan to serve as mentors and is designed to be used prior to actually becoming mentors. The instrument is divided into two sections. The first asks the teacher to summarize personal qualities and professional skills using a Likert-type scale. In the second section, the teacher uses the first section's descriptors to assess mentor preparation needs and to plan for acquiring additional skills and knowledge.

Massachusetts Teachers Association & Massachusetts Field Center for Teaching and Learning. (1990). *The first year.* Boston: Author.

In May 1990, The Massachusetts Teachers Association, in collaboration with the Massachusetts Field Center for Teaching and Learning, convened a group of first-year teachers to identify their needs. This is the 23-page report of the results of that process. The report is divided into two sections. The first summarizes the written and oral responses of the new teachers to open-ended questions about their preparation, experiences, successes, and failures. It then makes recommendations and offers advice to new teachers in general. The second section examines where the new teachers learned the skills and acquired the knowledge necessary to teach, and how they would redesign the components that went into their preparation. Of special interest to mentors are the new teachers' reactions to their introduction to the school community; their formal orientation; and their relationships with administrators, veteran teachers, school staff, the union, and parents.

Mezirow, J., & Associates (1990). *Fostering critical reflection in adulthood.* San Francisco: Jossey-Bass.

When confronting new learning situations, adults bring with them their past experiences, prejudices, and assumptions. Because of this, they often have difficulty seeing new alternatives and adapting to change. This publication presents some specific exercises for helping adult learners reexamine deeply ingrained ways of thinking. The methods presented are based on what the authors call critical reflection, which they describe as recognizing the assumptions underlying one's beliefs and behaviors and trying to judge and justify their rationality in relation to the new learning. In addition to discussing traditional ways to stimulate reflection, such as journal writing, the authors present several less familiar processes including metaphor analysis, videotape analysis, and conceptual mapping—a schematic device for representing the relationships among sets of concepts.

Newton, A., Bergstrom, K., Brennan, N., Dunne, K., Gilbert, C., Ibarguen, N., Perez-Selles, M., & Thomas, E. (1994). *Mentoring: A resource and training guide for educators.* Andover, MA: The Regional Laboratory for Educational Improvement of the Northeast and Islands.

This comprehensive training guide for mentoring was developed by staff from state education agencies in Maine, Massachusetts, New Hampshire, New York, and Vermont, and staff from The Regional Laboratory for Educational Improvement of the Northeast and Islands.

Eight school districts piloted the guidebook and provided feedback for its modification.

The publication contains five sections: (1) Understanding Critical Components of a Mentoring Program, (2) Developing a Mentoring Program, (3) Preparing Mentor Teachers, (4) Statistics and Stories, and (5) The Launch-Teacher Induction as the Crucial Stage of the Professional Development Journey. Each section briefly reviews the research and literature on that topic; suggests additional resources; and includes relevant activities supported by directions, handouts, and masters for overheads. Taken together, the 800 page loose-leaf compendium provides a systematic structure for planning, implementing, and sustaining a mentoring program in the public schools.

Torres-Guzman, M. E., & Goodwin, A. L. (1995). *Mentoring bilingual teachers* (Occasional Papers in Bilingual Education, No. 12). Washington D.C.: The National Clearinghouse for Bilingual Education.

After a brief discussion of mentoring, the paper reviews the history and nature of mentoring bilingual teachers, examining how and why such mentoring differs from mainstream models. It goes on to point out and discuss at length such salient issues as certification match. It examines the impact of content on the mentor-mentee relationship, highlights concerns about the language and culture of instruction, looks closely at the correlation between language and cognitive development, and touches on the issue of transformation and power relationships. Although the paper does not go into mentoring in other content areas, the principles discussed can be generalized to apply to most disciplines.

Resource B:
The Connecticut
Competency
Instrument (CCI)

The Connecticut Competency Instrument (CCI) was developed and validated during the late 1980s and early 1990s for the purpose of assessing the teaching competencies of a beginning teacher that are observable in the teacher's classroom.

There are several assumptions embodied in the holistic approach represented by the CCI that are important for mentors of new teachers to understand if they intend to use the instrument to inform their mentoring behaviors. These assumptions are:

- Effective teaching can take many forms.
- Critical dimensions of teacher performance that promote learning can be defined across diverse educational contexts.
- The competence of beginning teachers as decision makers can be differentiated from that of experienced teachers.
- Effective teaching is sensitive to cultural diversity.
- Effective teaching must be judged in the context of the teacher's objectives.
- Professional judgment is vital to teacher assessment.

The CCI consists of 10 indicators organized into three clusters of competencies that can be thought of holistically as aspects of the instructional process. The clusters are (a) management of the classroom environment, (b) instruction, and (c) assessment of students' understanding. In each of these areas, the focus of the instrument is primarily teacher behavior, but the impact on student behavior in the classroom is also critical.

Following is the text of the CCI, reprinted with permission from the Connecticut State Department of Education.

I. MANAGEMENT OF THE CLASSROOM ENVIRONMENT

IA. THE TEACHER PROMOTES A POSITIVE LEARNING ENVIRONMENT

The teacher is responsible for the nature and quality of teacher-student interactions in her or his classroom. The teacher's perception of students and their abilities directly affects students' responses, motivation, and achievement. The teacher's interactions with students should be positive and designed to enhance the learning environment. The beginning teacher, therefore, establishes and maintains a positive learning environment by creating a physical environment conducive to learning and maintaining both positive teacher-student and student-student interactions.

DEFINING ATTRIBUTES

There are three defining attributes of promoting a positive learning environment. They reflect the use of a variety of techniques for promoting positive teacher-student interactions and a physical environment that is conducive to learning:

(1) Rapport: The teacher establishes rapport with all students by demonstrating patience, acceptance, empathy and/or interest in students through positive verbal and non-verbal exchanges. The teacher avoids sarcasm, disparaging remarks, sexist and racial comments, scapegoating and physical abuse. The teacher also exhibits her or his own enthusiasm for the content and for learning and maintains a positive social and emotional atmosphere in the learning environment.

(2) Communication of expectations for academic achievement: The teacher creates a climate that encourages all students to achieve. Expectations for success may be explicitly verbalized or communi-

cated through the teacher's approach to assigning tasks, rewarding student effort and providing help and encouragement to all students.

(3) Physical environment: To the extent it is under her or his control, the teacher establishes a physical environment that is safe and conducive to learning.

IB. THE TEACHER MAINTAINS APPROPRIATE STANDARDS OF BEHAVIOR

Research shows that effective teachers use management practices that include concrete, functional and explicit rules and standards that are established early in the school year and maintained throughout the year. Fitting consequences should be applied to both appropriate and inappropriate behaviors. Teachers' standards or rules may vary, but their use in the management of behavior should assist in effectively facilitating the teaching-learning process in the classroom. The beginning teacher will maintain these standards through clear and consistent expectations for appropriate student behavior.

DEFINING ATTRIBUTE

There is one defining attribute for the process of maintaining appropriate standards for behavior:

(1) Rules and standards of behavior are maintained: Either through explicit statements of rules or through responses to student behavior, the teacher communicates and reinforces appropriate standards of behavior for the students. The teacher applies fitting consequences when student behavior is either appropriate (i.e., consistent with the standards) or inappropriate. Even though a teacher's standards may vary, they should have the effect of facilitating student learning. A pattern of appropriate behavior indicates that rules and standards have been previously communicated to the students. A pattern of inappropriate behavior indicates that rules and standards of behavior are not being maintained.

IC. THE TEACHER ENGAGES THE STUDENTS IN THE ACTIVITIES OF THE LESSON

The amount of time students spend on the tasks of the lesson is important because it is a reflection and outcome of the teacher's management and instructional skills. Research consistently shows that the amount of time students spend successfully engaged in activities relevant to the lesson objectives is positively related to student achievement. Conversely, time spent disengaged or off-task is associated with low achievement gains. This indicator assesses the engagement of students in the activities of the lesson.

DEFINING ATTRIBUTES

There are two defining attributes for engagement of students:

(1) Student engagement: The beginning teacher engages a clear majority (at least 80 percent) of the students in the activities of the lesson. Engagement is defined as students' involvement in lesson activities consistent with the teacher's expectations or directions. Although a high rate of engagement is expected, it is acceptable for students to be momentarily off-task from time to time during a lesson.

(2) Re-engagement: When any student is persistently off-task, the teacher must attempt to bring her/him back on task. A variety of strategies may be used. A teacher's attempt to re-engage a student need not be successful; however, when unsuccessful, the teacher must make additional attempts to re-engage the student.

ID. THE TEACHER EFFECTIVELY MANAGES ROUTINES AND TRANSITIONS

How teachers allocate and manage the administrative and organizational activities of the classroom has a direct bearing on the amount of time that is available for instruction, and the quality of that instruction. Whereas Indicator IC is concerned with the amount of instructional time in which students are actually engaged in learning activities, Indicator ID deals with how the teacher manages the non-instructional time. It is expected that the beginning teacher will effectively use the time allocated for instruction by managing routines and transitions to support the purposes of instruction.

Classroom routines are non-instructional, organizational, administrative or repetitive activities such as roll-taking, pencil-sharpening or the distribution of materials and equipment, although the latter may be in preparation for subsequent instruction. Transitions are non-instructional organizational or administrative moves from one classroom activity or context to another. Transitions may occur between instructional activities as well as between an instructional and a non-instructional activity.

DEFINING ATTRIBUTE

There is one defining attribute of the management of routines and transitions:

(1) Effectiveness: The teacher should provide effective routines and transitions that reflect planning, established norms and a sense of structure. When appropriate, resources and materials should be organized and available. In addition, the amount of time spent on routines and transitions should be appropriate for their purpose and the makeup of the class. Depending upon the nature and purpose of a routine or transition, proceeding too quickly may be as detrimental as taking too much time with the non-instructional activities.

II. INSTRUCTION

Assessor judgment about the acceptability of teacher performance on the instruction indicators rests heavily on the clarity of the teacher's objectives. Beginning teachers must have clear and specific objectives for their lessons or for all learning activities. (Indicators IIA, IIB, IIC, and IID relate directly to the lesson objective.) It is important, therefore, for beginning teachers to fully understand what the students are expected to learn and clearly convey that understanding to assessors through the Pre-Assessment Information Form and Pre-Observation Interview. The Post-Observation Interview gives teachers an opportunity to indicate any changes made in their objectives or activities during the course of the lesson, or any unexpected classroom occurrences that could impact the observation.

There are frequent references to lesson elements within the indicators of the instruction cluster. These are discrete parts of a lesson, the beginnings or endings of which may be indicated by a change in activity, topic, or instructional arrangement.

IIA. THE TEACHER PRESENTS APPROPRIATE LESSON CONTENT

Research shows that teaching is most effective when content is both accurate and at a level of difficulty or complexity appropriate for the learners. The competent beginning teacher should demonstrate mastery of the subject matter through the representation and delivery of accurate content. The content of the lesson should also be aligned with the objectives of the lesson. Content includes, but is not limited to, lesson materials, student discussion, activities, practice, modeling, demonstrations, teacher presentation, and teacher questioning.

DEFINING ATTRIBUTES

There are three defining attributes for assessing the lesson content:

(1) Choice of content: The content must be aligned with the lesson objectives. Teachers should not significantly deviate from the lesson content as specified in the objectives, unless the objectives or activities are modified during the lesson.

(2) Level of difficulty: The lesson content must be at a level of difficulty (neither too easy nor too hard) that is suitable for the level of students' cognitive development. Content should also be at an appropriate level for the students' social, emotional and/or physical development. The teacher will use vocabulary and language appropriate to the learners. The appropriate level of difficulty may differ among students, and often the appropriateness may be judged by student responses and behavior.

(3) Accuracy: The lesson content must be accurate. Infrequent, minor inaccuracies not significantly related to the content should not be considered in the rating of this defining attribute.

IIB. THE TEACHER CREATES A STRUCTURE FOR LEARNING

The beginning teacher is responsible for providing the structure in which learning occurs. A consistent research finding is that when teachers appropriately structure instructional information, student achievement is increased. Research shows that initiations facilitate student understanding. Research suggests that closures assist students in integrating and processing information, and practitioners and education specialists believe it is an important part of lesson structure. Lesson elements are discrete parts of a lesson, the beginnings or endings of which may be indicated by a change of activity, topic or instructional arrangement.

DEFINING ATTRIBUTES

There are two defining attributes of creating a structure for learning:

(1) Initiations: Initiations must relate to lesson objectives and help students anticipate or focus on the lesson content. The beginning teacher will provide initiations at the beginning of the lesson or between significant instructional elements throughout the lesson. Frequently, initiations preview what is to be learned, why it is to be learned, or how it relates to past or future learning. Initiations have a role in motivating students. Initiations may be explicit statements or may occur through established instructional activities or teacher modeling tied to the lesson objectives. Simply stating the activities in which the students will engage is not sufficient for initiation.

(2) Closures: Closures must relate to lesson objectives and help students understand the purpose of the lesson content. The beginning teacher is responsible for closure at the end of the lesson or between significant instructional elements throughout the lesson. Simply restating lesson objectives is not sufficient for closure.

IIC. THE TEACHER DEVELOPS THE LESSON TO PROMOTE ACHIEVEMENT OF THE LESSON OBJECTIVES

Development is the heart of the lesson and the key to establishing meaning for students and achieving lesson objectives. It is in developing the lesson that the teacher organizes instructional activities and materials to enhance students' learning of lesson content. Effective development motivates and moves students toward the lesson objectives. In an effectively developed lesson, related elements are manifestly linked to each other, and the materials and instructional arrangements contribute to the lesson's momentum. Lesson elements are discrete parts of a lesson, the beginnings or endings of which may be indicated by a change of activity, topic or instructional arrangement.

DEFINING ATTRIBUTES

There are two defining attributes of effective lesson development.

(1) Lesson development: Effective lesson development a) provides an underlying order within and among lesson elements, b) manifests a link between related lesson elements, and c) leads students to learn the content of each element.

Effective lesson development integrates these three components into a conceptual whole which establishes meaning for students and moves them toward achieving the lesson objective(s). The content of the lesson element(s) must be related to the lesson objective(s).

(2) Use of instructional arrangements and materials: Materials and instructional arrangements must purposefully support the development of the lesson. They should be used to promote student interest and involvement in the lesson.

IID. THE TEACHER USES APPROPRIATE QUESTIONING STRATEGIES

Questioning is an important aspect of instruction which stimulates and develops students' thinking and helps communicate what is to be learned. Questioning strategies also involve students, encourage the exchange of ideas or information between and among students and assist students in meeting the lesson objectives. Questioning may be explicit and verbal or may be implicitly embedded in lesson materials or activities. When using explicit questioning, the competent beginning teacher waits for and listens to student answers, effectively responds and incorporates those answers into the lesson. Questioning may be explicit and verbal or may be implicitly embedded in lesson materials or activities. Questioning includes any activity the teacher uses to obtain student oral, written or non-verbal responses to the content of the lesson.

DEFINING ATTRIBUTES

There are three defining attributes that are applied to assess questioning:

(1) Cognitive level: The level of questioning must be appropriate to the lesson objectives. If the teacher is seeking recall of basic facts or concepts, then questions of a lower cognitive level are appropri-

ate. If the teacher's purpose is to stimulate higher-level thinking, such as analysis and evaluation, then questions of a higher cognitive level are appropriate. In many lessons, a variety of questioning levels will be appropriate.

(2) Responding to students: The teacher should respond to student replies, failures to answer, questions and/or comments. Where appropriate, the teacher builds upon student contributions to work toward the lesson objectives. Responses may include waiting, clarifying, refocusing, acknowledging correct responses, providing corrective feedback, extending or prompting.

(3) Opportunities for student involvement: Opportunities for student involvement must be provided by allowing all students an opportunity to answer the question(s) and seeking answers from a variety of students. Opportunities may include student-initiated questions and tasks as well as teacher-initiated questions. Appropriate use of wait time allows all students an opportunity to become involved in questioning activity.

IIE. THE TEACHER COMMUNICATES CLEARLY, USING PRECISE LANGUAGE AND ACCEPTABLE ORAL EXPRESSIONS

The quality of teacher communication is important for student learning. Teachers should provide clear presentations and explanations of the lesson content. Precise communication and clear speech should serve to enhance student understanding. Teachers are expected to model acceptable oral expressions.

DEFINING ATTRIBUTES

There are three attributes that define acceptable teacher communication:

(1) Precision of communication: Precision of communication refers to the communication of meaning. The teacher must communicate in a coherent manner, avoiding vagueness and ambiguity that interfere with student understanding. Precision of communication includes giving directions.

(2) Clarity of speech: Clarity of speech refers to the technical quality of communication. This consists of the teacher's articulation,

volume and rate of delivery, which must not interfere with student understanding.

(3) Oral expressions: A pattern of unacceptable oral expressions must be avoided. Incorrect grammar and slang should be avoided; however, it is acceptable for teachers selectively to use current popular phrases or slang to make a point, establish rapport or enhance the learning. Vulgarity should be avoided.

III. ASSESSMENT [of student progress]

Assessor judgment about the acceptability of teacher performance on the assessment indicator rests heavily on the clarity of the teacher's objectives. Consequently beginning teachers must have clear and specific objectives for their lessons for all learning activities. It is important, therefore, for beginning teachers to fully understand what the students are expected to learn and to clearly convey that understanding to assessors through the Pre-Assessment Information Form and Pre-Observation Interview. The Post-Observation Interview gives teachers an opportunity to indicate any changes in planned objectives or activities made as a result of monitoring.

IIIA. THE TEACHER MONITORS STUDENT UNDERSTANDING OF THE LESSON AND ADJUSTS INSTRUCTION WHEN NECESSARY

The importance of monitoring and adjusting is underscored by research on teaching. More learning will occur when teachers regularly monitor their students' understanding and adjust instruction when appropriate. The two components support one another in promoting student understanding; appropriate adjustment is contingent upon sufficient monitoring and should not be viewed separately. The beginning teacher should monitor students' understanding at appropriate points in the lesson and adjust her or his teaching when the resulting information indicates it is necessary to do so. Lesson elements are discrete parts of a lesson, the beginnings or endings of which may be indicated by a change of activity, topic or instructional arrangement.

DEFINING ATTRIBUTES

The Indicator has two defining attributes:

(1) Monitoring for understanding: The purpose of monitoring is to see that students are understanding the lesson content and moving toward the lesson objectives. Toward this end, the teacher must check the level of understanding of a variety of students at appropriate points during the lesson. These points include (but are not limited to) the completion of a lesson element and after an adjustment resulting from monitoring.

(2) Adjusting when necessary: The teacher must use appropriate strategies to adjust his or her teaching when monitoring or spontaneous student response indicates that students are misunderstanding or failing to learn. Strategies for adjustment may include re-presenting information, re-explaining a concept, asking different types of questions, and/or slowing the pace of instruction. The teacher will also use appropriate strategies to adjust when monitoring indicates that students have mastered the concepts being taught. Such strategies may include accelerating the pace of instruction, providing enrichment activities, and/or moving on to new material. When monitoring indicates that adjustment is necessary but not possible within the lesson, the teacher must acknowledge to the students the need for adjustment at a later time.